The Gospel on the Ground

KRISTI MCLELLAND

Lifeway Press
Brentwood, Tennessee

Published by Lifeway Press® • © 2022 Kristi McLelland

Reprinted July 2022

All rights reserved. No part of this work may be reproduced or transmitted in any form or by any means, electronic or mechanical, including photocopying and recording, or by any information storage or retrieval system, except as may be expressly permitted in writing by the publisher. Requests for permission should be addressed in writing to Lifeway Press®; 200 Powell Place, Suite 100; Brentwood, TN 37027.

ISBN: 978-1-0877-4824-5

Item: 005833482

Dewey decimal classification: 270.1

Subject heading: CHURCH HISTORY—30–600, EARLY CHURCH / CHRISTIANITY / JESUS CHRIST

Unless otherwise noted all Scripture quotations are from THE HOLY BIBLE, NEW INTERNATIONAL VERSION®, NIV® Copyright © 1973, 1978, 1984, 2011 by Biblica, Inc.® Used by permission. All rights reserved worldwide. Scripture quotations marked (ESV) are from the ESV® Bible (The Holy Bible, English Standard Version®), copyright © 2001 by Crossway, a publishing ministry of Good News Publishers. Used by permission. All rights reserved.

To order additional copies of this resource, write Lifeway Resources Customer Service; 200 Powell Place, Suite 100; Brentwood, TN 37027; Fax order to 615.251.5933; call toll-free 800.458.2772; email orderentry@lifeway.com; or order online at lifeway.com.

Printed in the United States of America.

Lifeway Women Bible Studies
Lifeway Resources
200 Powell Place, Suite 100
Brentwood, TN 37027

IMAGE CREDITS: Page 14—Getty Images; Page 20—Getty Images; Page 47—Tribute Penny: Creative Commons; Page 52—Solomon's Temple: Illustrated by Dick Wahl; Page 74—Map provided by Holman Bible Atlas; Page 105—Terracotta Panathenaic prize amphora (jar) 550 BC: The Bothmer Purchase Fund, 197, Met collection, Public Domain; Page 118 (Top Image)—Triclinium Excavated in the House of Actaeon, Pompei: Met Collection, Public Domain, Bequest of Harry G. Sperling, 1971; (Bottom Image)—Triclinium Sketch: Shutterstock; Page 123—Map provided by Holman Bible Atlas; Page 124—Artemis of Ephesus Statue: Digital image courtesy of the Getty's Open Content Program; Page 149 (Top)—Illustrated by Dick Wahl; (Bottom)—Illustrated by Scott Burroughs; Page 174 (Middle)—Faith Crabtree; Page 175 (Top)—Illustrated by Laure Fournier; (Bottom)—Ship of Castor and Pollux: Met Collection, Public Domain, Bequest of Phyllis Massar, 2011; Page 190—Map provided by Holman Bible Atlas. All other images—Getty Images or the author's own.

EDITORIAL TEAM, LIFEWAY WOMEN BIBLE STUDIES

Becky Loyd
Director,
Lifeway Women

Tina Boesch
Manager

Chelsea Waack
Production Leader

Sarah Doss
Content Editor

Erin Franklin
Production Editor

Lauren Ervin
Graphic Designer

TABLE OF CONTENTS

- 4   **ABOUT THE AUTHOR**
- 5   **INTRODUCTION**
- 9   **HOW TO USE THIS STUDY**
- 12   **SESSION ONE:** Taking on the Teachings of Jesus—The Rabbi-Talmid Relationship
- 34   **SESSION TWO:** Taking on the Power of Jesus—The Kingdom of God Is a Mustard Seed
- 60   **SESSION THREE:** Kingdom of Celebration & Empire of Entertainment—Meaning Invades Meaninglessness
- 84   **SESSION FOUR:** Kingdom of Abundance & Empire of Scarcity—Subversive Generosity on the Move
- 108   **SESSION FIVE:** Kingdom of Togetherness & Empire of Separation—Orphans Find Sonship at the Table
- 134   **SESSION SIX:** Kingdom of Togetherness & Empire of Separation—Brothers and Sisters Bound Together in Prayer and Fasting
- 160   **SESSION SEVEN:** The Long Journey Home—Headed to the Father's House
- 183   **LEADER GUIDE**
- 187   **ACTS READING PLAN**
- 188   **ENDNOTES**
- 190   **MAP OF THE ROMAN EMPIRE**

ABOUT THE AUTHOR

Kristi McLelland is a speaker, teacher, and college professor. Since completing her Master of Arts in Christian Education at Dallas Theological Seminary, she has dedicated her life to discipleship, to teaching people how to study the Bible for themselves, and to writing about how God is better than we ever knew by explaining the Bible through a Middle Eastern lens. She has written another Bible study on Jesus's earthly ministry and His interactions with first-century women titled *Jesus and Women*. Her great desire for people to truly experience the love of God birthed a ministry in which she leads biblical study trips to Israel, Turkey, Greece, and Italy.

For more information about Kristi and what she's up to, visit: *newlensbiblicalstudies.com*.

INTRODUCTION

Every adventure begins in a moment, and the best ones come to us.

As we begin our study of *The Gospel on the Ground*, I want to share a bit about myself and my journey. In 2007, an adventure found me; the Lord opened the door for me to study the Bible in Egypt and Israel. During that time, I got to know the historical, cultural, linguistic, and geographical world of the Bible.

I was eating foods that Abraham ate, seeing stars in the sky that Jesus saw from earth when He looked up at night, and walking on ancient roads that Peter and Paul would have walked more than two thousand years ago. I learned to study and understand the Bible through the Middle Eastern lens (the way it would have been understood in Jesus's first-century world) rather than the Western lens that usually shapes the way we read God's Word in the United States today.

Studying the written Word of God in the living land of God where it all actually happened changed me forever. And here I am fourteen years later still talking about all I learned and all I continue to learn.

You may know that Jerusalem is considered the epicenter of the earth for the Jewish people. It's known as the city where God's name dwells. It's known as the city where God's temple stood during Solomon's reign and during the time of Jesus. *Yerushalayim*—the destination of all pilgrimage travel to the Holy Land for thousands of years.[1]

Jerusalem feels like home to me. I feel the most whole and centered when I am there. I feel God there—as I see the places where Jesus walked and as I occupy the incarnational spaces He once filled in His thirty-three years on earth.

As a Jewish man, Jesus would have visited Jerusalem a few times a year to observe the annual festivals according to the commands of God. In His adulthood, Jesus was known as a Galilean Rabbi because His family was from Galilee. He lived His whole life within the districts of Galilee, Samaria, and Judea. For the vast majority of His life, He never traveled outside of a one-hundred-mile radius from where He was born. Yet His name is spoken and known in every corner of the earth.

How can that be? How does a man who lived a relatively short life of just more than thirty years and who spent His time mostly within a one-hundred-mile radius change the entire world and the course of all of human history?

This "gospel on the ground" feast is the story of how this Jesus-centered, world transformation happened and how it is *still* happening in our world and in our lives today.

(If you've never studied the Bible with me before, you'll learn that I call our study times together "feasts" because we don't so much *read* the Word of God as we *eat* it. We take it in, and we let it do its work in us. More on that later.)

We've discussed how Jerusalem was important to the Jewish people during Jesus's time on earth and it remains so to this day.

Jerusalem is also important to us as the New Testament church, even now. And here's why: the church was birthed in Jerusalem—at God's house, the temple—during one of the three main annual foot festivals, Pentecost.

We find our beginning here—in Jerusalem at God's house. But the story of the Bible and the church doesn't end in Jerusalem.

Something began that day at Pentecost—something that is still underway today, in this very moment.

Something Jesus had told them to look for, to wait for . . .

> But you will receive power when the Holy Spirit comes on you; and you will be my witnesses in Jerusalem, and in all Judea and Samaria, and to the ends of the earth.
> **ACTS 1:8**

From Acts 1:8 on, the Bible tells the story of how God's fledgling church became His witnesses in all the earth by the power of the Holy Spirit. The gospel started moving along the ground, moving out from Jerusalem and into Judea, Samaria, and even further into the heart of the greater Greco-Roman world at that time. The early believers in Jesus carried the story of Jesus with them wherever they went.

And by the end of Acts, we're told that the gospel of Jesus and the way of Jesus, embodied in His followers, had made its way to another important city—the imperial city of the Roman Empire—Rome.

The kingdom of God started invading the empire of this world. And let me tell you, the way of Jesus and the way of Caesar could not have been more different. The empires of the world had been anchored in acquisition. The world's philosophy could be summed up with the phrase "if you are strong enough to take it, it's yours." When you consider the idea of empire, think of the power and glory of Egypt, Assyria, Babylon, Persia, Greece, and Rome in the first century. The world of empire prizes strength and using that strength to stay on top.

In contrast, we find the kingdom of God to be anchored in relinquishment. The way of Jesus says the last will be first. Jesus says we are to lose our lives to gain them. The way of the kingdom of God is entirely upside-down to the way of the world and empire. Caesar will do anything to stay on top. Jesus says the way to flourish is to go low.

As we'll explore together in this biblical feast, the story of the book of Acts and the early church can be summed up in a series of subversively sanctified invasions— God's redemptive work of grace confronting some of the seemingly insurmountable institutions of the world.

The kingdom of celebration invading the empire of entertainment.

The kingdom of abundance invading the empire of scarcity.

The kingdom of togetherness invading the empire of separateness.

I love the way that C. S. Lewis put it:

> Enemy-occupied territory—that is what this world is. Christianity is the story of how the rightful king has landed, you might say landed in disguise, and is calling us all to take part in a great campaign of sabotage.[2]
>
> C. S. LEWIS

This story continues today with us. We are being drafted into the "great campaign of sabotage" to spread the way and the wisdom of the reign of the rightful and benevolent King.[3]

Even now, you and I are being invited into the movement of the New Testament church as it grows, reaching unto the ends of the earth.

The kingdom of God is still coming down to the ground. And we, as God's people, are called to bring subversive celebration, abundance, and togetherness—light to a weary world that sometimes seems darker than anything else.

The witness of the women and men of the early church spoke to God's all-sufficient worth. And the witness of our lives remains potent, speaking a word to the empires of today.

So what do you say?

Will you step into the adventure God is calling you to? Will you let Him use you in this chapter of the church's story?

Our adventure can begin even at this moment.

Let's take hold of it together.

All the best,

Kurt V. McLelland

HOW TO USE THIS STUDY

In our time together, we are going to glimpse some snapshots of the early church, mostly living in a Greco-Roman world. We are going to study God's Word in a way that might seem a bit different from what you've experienced in the past. We are going to strive to view the Bible with a Middle Eastern lens and, at the same time, study a few Bible passages in a traditionally Jewish way—the way the rabbis would have taught Jesus the Bible and the way some rabbis still teach the children in Israel today.

With that in mind, let's discuss a bit of the philosophical framework for our study:

WE APPROACH THE SCRIPTURES AS CHILDREN EXPECTING TO BE FED BY OUR FATHER.

It can be easy to sit down with our Bibles and think something like, *OK, let me figure out some application from the passage I'm reading today.* I have good news for you—we are not spiritual orphans. We have a gracious heavenly Father who feeds us to the full with His Word; He gives abundantly. As we read the Word, we do our part by being open to what God will teach us. We posture ourselves to obey and to be gratefully fed by the living God through His Word and by the power of His Spirit. But God is in charge of feeding us.

WE'RE NOT LOOKING FOR THE "RIGHT" ANSWER.

Though it may sound strange to our Western ears, in Judaism, the student with all of the good questions is better than the student with all of the right answers. We never just read the Bible; we interact with it, asking questions of the text. We want to know what a text teaches us about God before we ask what it teaches us about ourselves. In our time together, we're going to focus on interacting with the biblical text in community, and we're going to learn to be OK with questions that cannot be easily answered and even questions that may leave us scratching our heads with a bit of mystery.

WE WANT GOD'S WORD TO BECOME A PART OF WHO WE ARE.

The Middle Eastern way of learning falls in line with more of an oral teaching tradition, less so the more formal learning style of our Western world. In our study together, we want these concepts in God's Word to get into our hearts and minds so much that they become a part of who we are, changing the way we see God and interact with the world. You'll notice we will revisit some of the same concepts each week; the study is intentionally crafted in this way. By the end of our time together, I hope these biblical concepts are so clear and familiar they are almost like second nature to you.

LEARNING WILL BE A COMMUNITY ENDEAVOR IN OUR TIME TOGETHER.

In the Middle Eastern way, learning is very communal. Here's what I mean: in a Middle Eastern context, it would be common to see rabbis teaching students as they walk down the road. This teaching tradition places significant value on students discussing an issue with one another. Rabbis often instruct their students to "go first" and discuss what they believe about a teaching before the teacher explains the concept to them. We're going to adopt some of those ideas in our time together. In many cases, I'll "go first" in our feast-teaching times. But you'll notice group discussion guides that I've crafted especially for you to use as you *yeshiva*, or discuss biblical texts together, after we begin unpacking them in our video teaching sessions.

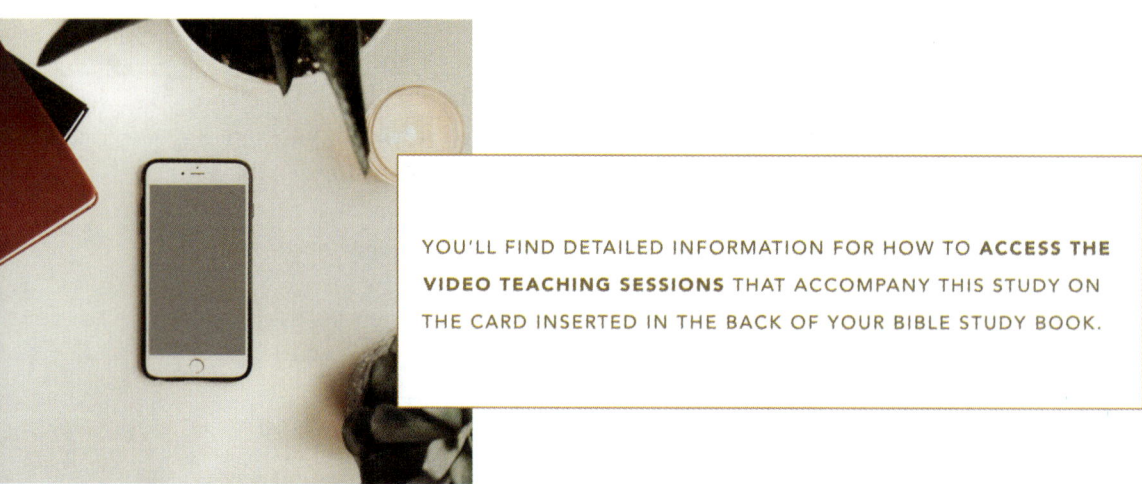

YOU'LL FIND DETAILED INFORMATION FOR HOW TO **ACCESS THE VIDEO TEACHING SESSIONS** THAT ACCOMPANY THIS STUDY ON THE CARD INSERTED IN THE BACK OF YOUR BIBLE STUDY BOOK.

Each session, you'll find the following sections:

The **Watch** section

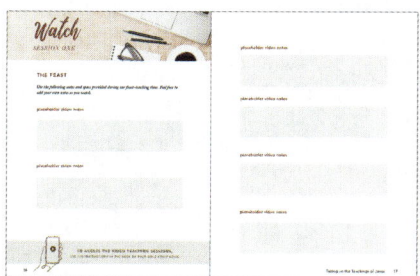

The **Discuss** section

The **Follow-Up** section

The **Look** section

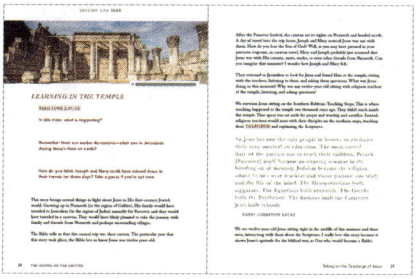

The **Learn** section

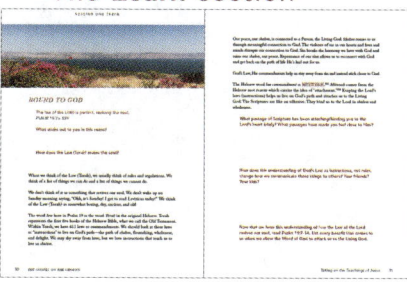

The **Live** section

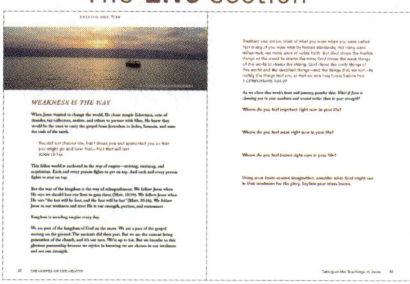

The "Watch" and "Discuss" times are meant to be completed with your small group. But the "Follow-up," "Look," "Learn," and "Live" sections are for your personal study time. Instead of labeling them by days of study, we've labeled them by sections. Feel free to complete each between our weekly group times as you see fit throughout the week. Please note, terms in the text marked with THIS STYLE are explained in further detail in the glossary found on *lifeway.com/gospelontheground*.

11

Taking on the Teachings of Jesus

THE RABBI-TALMID RELATIONSHIP

SESSION ONE

I'm a professor. At the beginning of every class each semester, I usually tell my college students a few important things. I'll share one of them with you: *The Bible is not only the best story that's ever been told; it's also the truest story that's ever been told.*

The things we read about in the Word of God happened.

Remember, we do not just want to know the Word of God. We want to eat it. We want to take it in like a feast and let it do its work in us. We want it to become part of us so we can carry the Word with us wherever we go.

The Word of God is like great food. Great food is best experienced with great people. In Jesus's world, the Bible was experienced communally first and individually second. In calling His disciples and building His kingdom, Jesus was forming a new covenant people who would not only know what He knows, but be just like Him. Not just in word. But in word and deed.

This seven-session study is a feast to be eaten together as we take a journey through some of the book of Acts. The Word of God is living and active and so are we as God's children. When any believer sits down with a Bible, it is life with life. As we study His Word, the life that God has placed in us through His Holy Spirit interacts with the living Word of God to create more life in us—abundant life, an overflow of life—because God is the Author of life.

The Word is on the move. The kingdom is on the move. As followers of Jesus, we can't help but be on the move too.

As we journey through the Bible, the book of Acts, and beyond, we will journey together. In antiquity, no one traveled alone. If you traveled alone in that world, you got jacked. You could easily be attacked. Jesus told a parable in Luke 10:30-37; we call it the parable of the good Samaritan. This parable follows a man who traveled alone, and as you may remember, he got jacked! In Jesus's time, you always traveled in a caravan. Usually many families traveled together, helping and aiding one another along the way to their destinations.

We will travel the pages of the Bible together. We will welcome the adventure that is upon us, to live it out—together. So in our own way, we are a caravan.

As we begin our feast and our journey, take a few moments to answer the following questions before you watch the video teaching.

Why did you say yes to this feast and journey?

What are you asking the Lord to do in your life through this seven-session feast and journey?

Finish the following sentence:

"I am here because my heart needs _____."

Who is in your caravan? Who are you feasting with and journeying with through this seven-session adventure?

Watch
SESSION ONE

THE FEAST

Use the following notes and space provided during our feast-teaching time. Feel free to add your own notes as you watch.

Jesus spent the vast majority of His life within a one-hundred-mile radius of where He was born. Yet His name is spoken and known in every corner of the earth. This is the story of how it happened—and is still happening.

The Greeks loved knowledge. The Romans loved power. The Hebrews have always loved the light.

The kingdom of God faces outward. The kingdom of God is on the move.

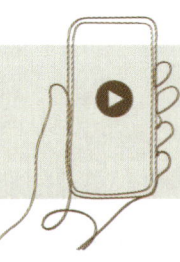

TO ACCESS THE VIDEO TEACHING SESSIONS,
USE THE INSTRUCTIONS IN THE BACK OF YOUR BIBLE STUDY BOOK.

Education and stages of life in a typical Jewish male:

In the first-century Jewish world, people chose their rabbis. Jesus came on the scene and started choosing His disciples.

As a great one (rabbi), He reached for people, invited them to follow Him. In choosing His disciples, Jesus was not saying, "I think you can learn what I know." He was saying, "I think you can be just like me."

We come into this world looking for a face. Discipleship, then and now, is Jesus looking us in our faces and inviting us to follow Him.

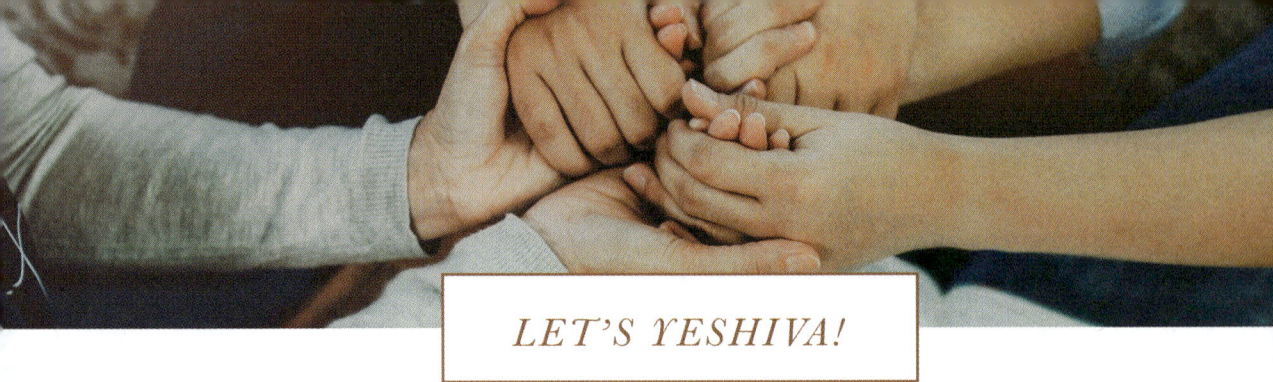

LET'S YESHIVA!

Both learning and travel were done best in community in the biblical world. We want to practice YESHIVA together—discussing, workshopping, and brainstorming around what we heard in this session's video teaching.

As we already briefly discussed, safe travel in antiquity was done in caravans. Families would walk together during the day and stop for rest and sleep at night on the way. As they settled in for the night, they would usually share stories by firelight and eat their food, resting from the long day's journey. Storytelling was the main source of entertainment in the biblical world. They told famous stories, funny stories, sad stories, real stories—their stories. They got to know each other as they journeyed and ate together.

Now that we have feasted on our first video teaching, take some time to discuss the following questions with your group. We're going to learn from each other by journeying together and sharing some of our own stories during this seven-session feast.

What did you just hear or see in our feast together that you want to remember?

What's the most encouraging thing that you learned this week about the rabbi-disciple relationship in the first-century world of Jesus?

We come into this world looking for a face. What was your first thought when you heard that statement during the teaching?

session one **follow-up**

WHOM DOES THE LIVING GOD CHOOSE?

Jesus was highly unusual in His first-century Jewish world as a "great one" (**RABBI**) who went out and chose His disciples. In a world where it was the highest honor to be able to come under the yoke of a rabbi and walk with him, Jesus, the "great one" (rabbi), did the work of seeing, choosing, and inviting people to follow Him and learn to be just like Him. He knew that while He would live most of His earthly life within a one-hundred-mile radius of where He was born, His disciples would be the ones to carry the gospel to the very ends of the earth. He knew *we* would *still* be carrying it to this day.

In choosing His disciples, Jesus was acting like His heavenly Father.

At the very beginning of the biblical story, there was another choosing—all the way back to the *genesis* (meaning *beginning*). The living God created Eden as a place of *shalom*—a place of wholeness, flourishing, harmony, and delight. Sin entered the story in Genesis 3 and *shalom* was lost, fractured, darkened, and marred. The living God would begin the ancient and ever work of bringing deep salvation, restoration, renewal, and redemption to the broken world. *But whom would He choose to partner with Him in this great restoration work?*

> *Shalom*
> A place of wholeness, flourishing, harmony, and delight.

READ GENESIS 12:1-4 AND 15:1-6.

What did God promise to Abram?

List any information we're given about Abram's life in these passages.

Taking on the Teachings of Jesus

> GOD CHOSE ABRAM AND TOLD HIM THAT HE WOULD MAKE HIM INTO ABRAHAM—AN EXALTED FATHER OF A MULTITUDE.

In the ancient world of patriarchy, males with strength and numbers ruled from the top. Men with lots of children were prized, honored, exalted, and valued. Impotence and barrenness were both considered curses.

We would expect the Lord to pick a "great father" to partner with Him. But He chose a seventy-five-year-old man with zero children (Gen. 12:1-4). He chose Abram. Being a seventy-five-year-old childless male in the ancient world would have been laughable. Abram would have been seen as the epitome of weakness. He was like a blank slate in society's eyes. No one in that world would have chosen Abram. But the living God did. God chose Abram and told him that He would make him into Abraham—an exalted father of a multitude.

The living God wasn't done choosing yet.

In the ancient world, the firstborn male was of supreme significance, highly desired, and favored. According to Torah Law, the firstborn received a double-portion of the inheritance (Deut. 21:15-17). The firstborn was seen as the picture of strength, power, and virility—everything prized in that world. The picture we get of Cain, Ishmael, and Esau in the book of Genesis points to strength.

But when we read Genesis, the living God kept choosing the second-born sons, not the firstborn sons.

It's not Cain. It's Abel.

It's not Ishmael. It's Isaac.

It's not Esau. It's Jacob.

The living God was not afraid to choose a seventy-five-year-old impotent male, and He was not afraid to choose second-born sons in a world where firstborn sons held all the strength and preeminence.

The living God still wasn't done choosing.

For women in antiquity, barrenness was considered a type of curse. It was shameful to be unable to bring forth children into the world, to add to the family, the clan, and the tribe. As a woman in antiquity, you would rather be anything but barren. Being barren was figuratively considered the bottom of the barrel. We would expect the living God to choose fertile women, with babies popping out here, there, and everywhere.

But when we read Genesis, the living God kept choosing barren women to be the wives of the patriarchs! *Whaaaaaaat?*

Abraham's wife Sarah was barren.

Isaac's wife Rebekah was barren.

Jacob's wife Rachel was barren.

When the living God was choosing whom He wanted to partner with to change the world, He chose impotent men, second-born sons, and barren women. Three times over He chose those no one else would have ever chosen.

The Bible was given to us so that we might know who the living God is—what He's like and what it is to walk with Him.

The biblical record tells us that you don't have to be powerful in plenty, strong in might, or fertile in production for the living God to choose you. Jesus knew this, and He chose like His heavenly Father did.

Jesus chose simple fishermen, "sons of thunder" (Mark 3:17), tax collectors, zealots, and others to be His followers. And Jesus chooses you.

> **If you are a follower of Jesus, do you really believe Jesus has chosen you? Explain.**

> **How would you act differently if you walked every day of your life with a full sense of God's choosing you?**

session one **look**

✸ Temple at Capernaum as it appears today

LEARNING IN THE TEMPLE

READ LUKE 2:41-52.

In this story, what is happening?

Remember from our earlier discussions—what was in Jerusalem during Jesus's time on earth?

How do you think Joseph and Mary could have missed Jesus in their travels? Take a guess if you're not sure.

This story brings several things to light about Jesus in His first-century Jewish world. Growing up in Nazareth (in the region of Galilee), His family would have traveled to Jerusalem (in the region of Judea) annually for Passover, and they would have traveled in a caravan. They would have likely planned to take the journey with family and friends from Nazareth and perhaps surrounding villages.

The Bible tells us that this annual trip was their custom. The particular year that this story took place, the Bible lets us know Jesus was twelve years old.

After the Passover festival, the caravan set its sights on Nazareth and headed north. A day of travel into the trip home, Joseph and Mary noticed Jesus was not with them. How do you lose the Son of God? Well, as you may have guessed in your previous response, in caravan travel, Mary and Joseph probably just assumed that Jesus was with His cousins, aunts, uncles, or even other friends from Nazareth. Can you imagine that moment? I wonder how Joseph and Mary felt.

They returned to Jerusalem to look for Jesus and found Him at the temple, sitting with the teachers, listening to them, and asking them questions. What was Jesus doing at this moment? Why was any twelve-year-old sitting with religious teachers at the temple, listening, and asking questions?

We envision Jesus sitting on the southern rabbinic teaching steps. This is where teaching happened at the temple two thousand years ago. They didn't teach inside the temple. That space was set aside for prayer and worship and sacrifice. Instead, religious teachers would meet with their disciples on the southern steps, teaching their TALMIDIM and explaining the Scriptures.

> Please note, terms in the text marked with THIS STYLE are explained in further detail in the glossary found at *lifeway.com/gospelontheground*.

So Jews became the only people in history to predicate their very survival on education. The most sacred duty of the parents was to teach their children. Pesach [Passover] itself became an ongoing seminar in the handing on of memory. Judaism became the religion whose heroes were teachers and whose passion was study and the life of the mind. The Mesopotamians built ziggurats. The Egyptians built pyramids. The Greeks built the Parthenon. The Romans built the Coliseum. Jews built schools.[1]

RABBI JONATHAN SACKS

We see twelve-year-old Jesus sitting right in the middle of this moment and these men, interacting with them about the Scriptures. I really love this story because it shows Jesus's aptitude for the biblical text, as One who would become a Rabbi.

* Aerial view of Capernaum as it appears today

One way of understanding this moment in Jesus's life is that He was possibly preparing for His BAR MITZVAH that would happen the following year when He turned thirteen.

Age thirteen is a special year for both boys and girls in the Jewish faith and practice. It is a transitional year. At age thirteen for Jewish boys and age twelve for Jewish girls, they take part in a special and sacred ceremony. It is called a bar mitzvah for boys and BAT MITZVAH for girls. *Bar* means "son" and *mitzvah* means "commandment." Bar mitzvah literally means "son of the commandment." *Bat* means "daughter." Bat mitzvah literally means "daughter of the commandment."[2]

Most boys and girls celebrate this coming of age time with their families and friends in a party close to home. But some wealthy families have the means to take the party on the road and travel with friends and family to host their sons' bar mitzvah celebrations in Jerusalem. Jewish families come from all over the world for this celebration.

One of my favorite things to do when I take teams to Israel is to spend Mondays or Thursdays in Jerusalem at the temple area. Why? Because Mondays and Thursdays are bar mitzvah days!

In case you've never seen it, here's a quick snapshot.

Imagine this: *A thirteen-year-old boy is placed under a canopy and proceeds to the Kotel area, the Western Wall. He usually wears black pants with a white shirt. He wears a* kippah *or* yarmulke, *a small hat, on his head.*

The procession is loud and full of joy, life, and levity. Drummers go before the boy, playing their drums and singing into portable microphone systems. The family walks, dances, and sings with and behind the boy as he walks to the place where he will recite a portion of the Torah—the very moment he takes the commandments on for himself.

This time is a rite of passage for Jewish boys and girls. It is sacred and holy. It is bursting with celebration. The ceremony is followed by tons of food and family time. The ceremony is a memorial marker in the young boy's life. He lives forward from it as a man. A man of the commandments—God's commandments.

We can only imagine what Jesus's trip to Jerusalem would have looked like the year after this Luke 2 story occurred—the year He went up to Jerusalem as a thirteen-year-old. The bar mitzvah celebration as we see it in the Jewish faith today likely came into being much later than the first-century world of Jesus. But He and His family would have marked the milestone of His coming to the age of accountability and taking on His own spiritual growth. His family and friends would have surrounded Him and celebrated as He took the commandments onto Himself. I imagine singing, dancing, food, and more food.

The southern steps where the rabbis taught are still there today. In Israel, I take teams to sit on those steps as we unpack the biblical stories that happened on those very steps.

Peter preached his Pentecost message while standing on those steps. (See Acts 2.)[3]

The gospel started moving on the ground from that very place at Pentecost.

✳ The southern steps where the rabbis taught are still there today.

A few chapters later, we read that Stephen preached and the religious leaders responded by stoning him. Stephen will forever be the first Jewish-Christian MARTYR. (You'll read about it soon in Acts 7.)

Taking on the Teachings of Jesus   27

FORTY DAYS WITH JESUS

READ ACTS 1:1-3.

Focusing on verse 3, list the things the Bible says Jesus did after His resurrection.

What do you think "speaking about the kingdom of God" practically looked or sounded like (v. 3, ESV)?

Why do you think Jesus focused so much on the kingdom of God?

You only have to read the first three verses of the book of Acts to know it's about to be a wild ride, an incredible story, and an earth-changing adventure. Acts begins with the resurrected Jesus walking around for forty days giving "many convincing proofs that he was alive" (v. 3).

Can you imagine this? Can you imagine witnessing the crucifixion or even hearing about it from friends or family who witnessed it and then seeing the living Jesus walking down a Jerusalem street? Not once. Not twice. But for forty days.

I read these first three verses and questions flood my imagination and heart.

What did Jesus look like after the resurrection?

What was His demeanor?

What were those "convincing proofs" that He was alive (v. 3)?

Were people freaked out?

Were they astonished and afraid?

How did His mother Mary feel the first time she saw Him resurrected, back from the dead and forever victorious? Did she cry? Or laugh? Or both? What in the world was going on in her heart when she saw Him? Did He pick her up and twirl her around? Did He walk with His arm around her? Did she touch His hands, feet, and side?

I honestly cannot imagine being alive during those forty days and seeing the resurrected Jesus walking, talking, eating, and laughing—just living His final days on earth after shattering death forever.

We often see the number forty in the Bible. The flood lasted for forty days. The Israelites wandered in the desert for forty years. Goliath taunted the Israelites in the Elah Valley for forty days before David knocked his block off and chopped Goliath's head off with his own sword. Jesus was in the wilderness for forty days between His baptism and His emergence as a Rabbi of the Galilee. And here, at the beginning of Acts, we see forty once again.[4]

When you see forty in the Bible, look for change. Something's about to pivot in the story. It's an incredible beginning to the book of Acts.

Three verses in and you are already hooked. You have to keep reading. Where does *this* story go from here? For all our questions as to what it might have been like, we do know one detail in the story. We know what Jesus was talking about during those forty days. "He appeared to them over a period of forty days and spoke about the kingdom of God" (Acts 1:3).

Jesus knew He was about to ascend to heaven, and He also knew the gospel was about to move along the ground through these people from Jerusalem to Judea, Samaria, and unto the ends of the earth. Salvation had been won for all who would believe, but the world did not know it yet. Jesus knew they could not take this adventure without divine help and supernatural empowerment to embody and share the gospel (good news).

He not only walked around for forty days; He gave them their next instructions. "'Do not leave Jerusalem, but wait for the gift my Father promised, which you have heard me speak about. For John baptized with water, but in a few days you will be baptized with the Holy Spirit'" (vv. 4-5).

At our next feast-teaching video, we will pick up our story here—with Pentecost and the gift of the Holy Spirit poured out at a Jewish festival.

session one **learn**

BOUND TO GOD

> The law of the LORD is perfect, reviving the soul.
> **PSALM 19:7a, ESV**

What sticks out to you in this verse?

How does the Law (Torah) revive the soul?

When we think of the Law (Torah), we usually think of rules and regulations. We think of a list of things we can do and a list of things we cannot do.

We don't think of it as something that revives our souls. We don't wake up on Sunday morning saying, "Ohh, it's Sunday! I get to read Leviticus today!" We think of the Law (Torah) as somewhat boring, dry, ancient, and old.

The word *law* here in Psalm 19 is the word *Torah* in the original Hebrew.[5] Torah represents the first five books of the Hebrew Bible, what we call the Old Testament. Within Torah, we have 613 laws or commandments. We should look at these laws as "instructions" to live on God's path—the path of *shalom*, flourishing, wholeness, and delight. We may shy away from laws, but we love instructions that teach us to live in *shalom*.

30 THE GOSPEL ON THE GROUND

Our peace, our *shalom*, is connected to a Person, the living God. *Shalom* comes to us through meaningful connection to God. The violence of sin in our hearts and lives and minds disrupts our connection to God. Sin breaks the harmony we have with God and ruins our *shalom*, our peace. Repentance of our sins allows us to reconnect with God and get back on the path of life He's laid out for us.

God's Law, His commandments, help us stay away from sin and instead stick closer to God.

The Hebrew word for *commandment* is MITZVAH.[5] *Mitzvah* comes from the Hebrew root *tzavta* which carries the idea of "attachment."[6] Keeping the Lord's laws (instructions) helps us live on God's path and attaches us to the living God. The Scriptures are like an adhesive. They bind us to the Lord in *shalom* and wholeness.

What passage of Scripture has been attaching/binding you to the Lord's heart lately? What passages have made you feel close to Him?

How does this understanding of God's Law as instructions, not rules, change how we communicate these things to others? Your friends? Your kids?

Now that we have this understanding of *how* the Law of the Lord revives our soul, read Psalm 19:7-14. List every benefit that comes to us when we allow the Word of God to attach us to the living God.

session one **live**

* Fishing boat on the Sea of Galilee

WEAKNESS IS THE WAY

When Jesus wanted to change the world, He chose simple fishermen, "sons of thunder" (Mark 3:17), tax collectors, zealots, and others to partner with Him. He knew they would be the ones to carry the gospel from Jerusalem to Judea, Samaria, and unto the ends of the earth.

> You did not choose me, but I chose you and appointed you so that you might go and bear fruit—fruit that will last.
> JOHN 15:16a

This fallen world is anchored in the way of empire—striving, straining, and acquisition. Each and every person fights to get to the top. And each and every person fights to stay on top.

But the way of the kingdom is the way of relinquishment. We follow Jesus when He says we should lose our lives to gain them (Matt. 10:39). We follow Jesus when He says "the last will be first, and the first will be last" (Matt. 20:16). We follow Jesus in our weakness and trust He is our strength, portion, and sustenance.

Kingdom is invading empire every day.

We are part of the kingdom of God on the move. We are a part of the gospel moving on the ground. The ancients did their part. But we are the current living generation of the church, and it's our turn. We're up to bat. But we breathe in this glorious partnership because we rejoice in knowing we are chosen in our weakness and not our strength.

Brothers and sisters, think of what you were when you were called. Not many of you were wise by human standards; not many were influential; not many were of noble birth. But God chose the foolish things of the world to shame the wise; God chose the weak things of the world to shame the strong. God chose the lowly things of this world and the despised things—and the things that are not—to nullify the things that are, so that no one may boast before him.
1 CORINTHIANS 1:26-29

As we close this week's feast and journey, ponder this: *What if Jesus is choosing you in your weakness and wound rather than in your strength?*

Where do you feel impotent right now in your life?

Where do you feel weak right now in your life?

Where do you feel barren right now in your life?

Using your Spirit-soaked imagination, consider what God might use in that weakness for His glory. Explain your ideas below.

Taking on the Power of Jesus

THE KINGDOM OF GOD IS A MUSTARD SEED

SESSION TWO

Last week we learned about the importance of the rabbi-*talmid* (the word used for *disciple*) relationship in Jesus's first-century world.[1] Remember, disciples at that time didn't just want to know what their rabbi knew; they wanted to be just like him, and Jesus was unique in His world in the way He chose His disciples!

The early followers of Jesus would have understood the traditional *talmid* and rabbi relationship. They knew as they moved from Jerusalem to Judea, Samaria, and unto the ends of the earth that they would teach Jesus's teachings and do some of the very things Jesus did during His time with them on earth.

This week we'll pick up the storyline as Jesus instructed His disciples to wait in Jerusalem for the gift of the Holy Spirit. Divine word would need divine fire to fuel it. Being like Jesus throughout the Greco-Roman world would not only require knowing Jesus's teachings but receiving divine enablement to be like Him in the earth.

Much was to come, and they would not be able to sustain the work, persevere, or maintain joy in the adventure without the flame of God's Spirit burning inside of them. Pentecost would light them up; the Greco-Roman world would soon see their glow and be changed by it forever.

The church was birthed in Acts 2 during the Jewish festival called Shavuot (a Hebrew term). We often refer to it as Pentecost (a Greek term). We are getting ready to read and understand this epic moment in the story of the Bible, anchored in its Jewish historical and cultural context. So much more was happening at Pentecost than we know. Buckle up. It is good news.

While Jesus spent the majority of His life within a one-hundred-mile radius of where He was born, His disciples would carry the gospel on the ground here, there, and everywhere. They would end up in places like Ephesus, Corinth, Philippi, and Colossae. At the close of the book of Acts, Paul was in the imperial city—Rome herself. The gospel would take Jesus's followers further than they ever imagined. It would cost them more than they ever knew. On this adventure, God would use them to invade the Roman Empire with His very own kingdom.

As they went, they carried a particular teaching of Jesus in their Spirit-lit hearts. Jesus described the kingdom of God as a mustard seed (Matt. 13:31-32). We are getting ready to learn what He meant by that in His Jewish world in the land of Israel. It was a teaching, a truth, an image, and a reality they would never forget.

The story is about to get gospel-gorgeous.

As we begin our feast and our journey, take a few moments to answer the following questions before you watch the video teaching.

What have you been pondering since last week's feast?

What are the things you learned last week that you have been sharing with others?

READ ACTS 2:1-13.

As we head into Acts 2 and Pentecost, how would you currently describe or explain what happened at Pentecost?

Where did Pentecost happen?

What were they doing at Pentecost?

What were they reading during Pentecost?

✳ A flock of sheep graze in the woods at the Mount of Olives in Jerusalem

Watch
SESSION TWO

#GospelOnTheGround

THE FEAST

Use the following notes and space provided during our feast-teaching time. Feel free to add your own notes as you watch.

Jesus spent the vast majority of His life within a one-hundred-mile radius of where He was born. Yet His name is spoken and known in every corner of the earth. This is the story of how it happened—and is still happening.

Acts 1–8:3 happen in Jerusalem. Acts 8:4–11 primarily happen in Judea and Samaria. Acts 12–28 happen in the ends of the earth, the Greco-Roman Empire.

Acts 2 is the genesis, the beginning of the New Testament church.

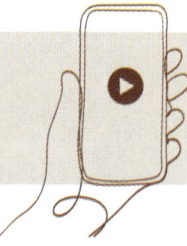

TO ACCESS THE VIDEO TEACHING SESSIONS,
USE THE INSTRUCTIONS IN THE BACK OF YOUR BIBLE STUDY BOOK.

Agricultural festivals (foot festivals): Passover, Festival of Unleavened Bread (spring); Pentecost, Feast of Weeks (spring); Festival of Tabernacles (fall)

In Acts 7, we have the first story of a martyr in the New Testament church. His name was Stephen.

Jesus likened the kingdom of God to a mustard seed. As Westerners we look at the form (size of the seed). As Middle Easterners, they look at the function (what the seed does).

The kingdom of celebration started invading the empire of entertainment.

session two **discuss**

LET'S YESHIVA!

We covered a lot of ground this week. Acts is an action-packed book in the story of the Bible. It's time to *yeshiva* and hear what everyone in your group is gleaning, adding, learning, and pondering after our second video teaching.

Take some time to discuss the following questions with your group:

What did you hear or see in our feast together that you want to remember?

How has your understanding of Acts 2 and what happened at Pentecost changed?

Jesus likened the kingdom of God to a mustard seed. How would this parable have encouraged the early followers of Jesus as they were "scattered" from Jerusalem to Judea, Samaria, and unto the ends of the earth? How does it encourage you today in your life and world?

Do you feel like you are currently participating more in the kingdom of celebration or the empire of entertainment? Why?

session two **follow-up**

TAMID SACRIFICES

READ ACTS 2:1-2.

Write the passage below.

Maybe you, like me, have imagined the events of Pentecost happening in a person's home. Acts 2:2 actually says they were sitting in a "house" when the Holy Spirit came upon them. As we look at Pentecost and how the Jewish people participated and celebrated this festival, we begin to get a more historical picture of where this story most likely happened.

First, Pentecost, also known as Shavuot (in Hebrew) or the Feast of Weeks, was one of the three pilgrimage festivals commanded by the Lord in Leviticus 23 and Deuteronomy 16. Remember, they were also known as the "foot festivals." Three times a year, the Jewish people would travel to Jerusalem (if they had the financial means and the physical ability) to meet at the temple and celebrate God's faithfulness in their lives. The living God was inviting them to His house in Jerusalem to celebrate with Him.

Pilgrims would not have traveled to Jerusalem to hang out in their families' homes. Instead they came to hang out at God's house with God's people. We tend to call it a "temple," but the Lord almost always refers to it as His house. The Lord loves His family and was inviting His covenant children to come and celebrate with Him during Pentecost. At these annual festivals, we imagine throngs of people gathering at God's house. It probably would have felt like the world's biggest family reunion at each festival.

Acts 2:1 said that "they were all together in one place." The only "house" in Jerusalem at that time big enough to hold thousands of pilgrims would have been God's house, the temple.[2]

The text of Acts 2 gives us another hint that the disciples of Jesus were at the temple together at Pentecost. And this hint is gospel-gorgeous!

> **Pentecost**
>
> One of the three pilgrimage festivals commanded by the Lord in Leviticus 23 and Deuteronomy 16.

✳ The model of Jerusalem in the second temple period of AD 66. At the center is the temple mount.

Taking on the Power of Jesus

Later in Acts 2, Peter stood up and addressed the crowd of folks who witnessed the followers of Jesus speaking in their "own language" as they were filled with the Holy Spirit. Some of the people alleged that the followers of Jesus were babbling because they were drunk. Peter's response sheds significant light on the location of the events during Pentecost.

In Acts 2:15, he said, "These people are not drunk, as you suppose. It's only nine in the morning!" 9:00 a.m. was a very specific time at the temple in Jerusalem. Each and every day at the temple, a lamb was sacrificed at both 9:00 a.m. and 3:00 p.m. These sacrifices were called the "TAMID sacrifices." *Tamid* means "continual, perpetual."[3] These two daily sacrifices were part of temple life and practice in the first-century world of Jesus and His followers.

In Exodus 29:38-42, the Lord instructed His people to offer these two daily/*tamid* sacrifices. They were known as the "morning sacrifice" at 9:00 a.m. and the "evening sacrifice" at 3:00 p.m. They were daily sacrifices of atonement, offered to make the community clean and holy before God. They were given as a way to tell God they were sorry for their sins (the ways they had walked contrary to God's laws) and they desired to be set back into right fellowship and communion with Him—back on the path of *shalom*. Ezra 3:3 mentions these daily sacrifices. The people had returned from exile in Persia and immediately built an altar on its foundation and began offering "the morning and evening sacrifices."

> "LOOK, THE LAMB OF GOD, WHO TAKES AWAY THE SIN OF THE WORLD!"
> JOHN 1:29b

We don't envision Peter's address to the crowd happening in a person's home. A home in those days would have been much too small to host such a large group. Instead, we envision them all at the temple, at God's house, during the time of the "morning sacrifice" at 9:00 a.m.

Now here's where it gets gospel-gorgeous.

In John 1:29, John the Baptist referred to Jesus as the "Lamb of God." He saw Jesus coming, and he proclaimed to his own followers, "Look, the Lamb of God, who takes away the sin of the world!" This perfect Lamb, Jesus, would later lay down His life as a sacrifice.

How would He do it? On a cross.

When would He do it? Let's take a look.

The Scriptures provide an incredibly specific timeline for the crucifixion of Jesus. It's so specific that it seems odd at first glance. Jesus was crucified indeed. Why do we need to know such an exact timetable?

READ MARK 15:25.

Record it below, circling any phrases or words that hint at the time of day.

Read the Matthew passage below. Circle any phrases or words that indicate time of day.

About three in the afternoon Jesus cried out in a loud voice . . .
And when Jesus had cried out again in a loud voice, he gave up his spirit.
MATTHEW 27:46a,50

Jesus was fulfilling once and for all *both* the morning sacrifice at 9:00 a.m. and the evening sacrifice at 3:00 p.m. The *tamid* sacrifices were completed in Him at His crucifixion. No longer would God require lambs to be perpetually or continually sacrificed before the Lord to atone for sin. Jesus is the forever *tamid* sacrifice, and His sacrifice is still providing salvation for all who believe in its atoning work on their behalf.

On the morning of the crucifixion, Jesus was placed on the cross at the exact same time the morning lamb was being sacrificed in the temple. I wonder if He could hear the bleating of the lambs. And Jesus gave up His spirit at the exact same time as the evening lamb was being sacrificed in the temple. Again, I often wonder if He could hear the bleating of the lambs.

So let's read John the Baptist's words once more in light of Jesus fulfilling the *tamid* sacrifices.

Look, the Lamb of God, who takes away the sin of the world!
JOHN 1:29b

Record a prayer of praise to our God whose sacrifice allows us to be His children for now and always.

session two **look**

✴ Mustard field in northern Israel

A TALE OF TWO KINGS

READ LUKE 3:1-2.

Record the names of the rulers listed in the passage along with their respective roles.

Ruler	Role

The book of Acts can be understood as the story of kingdom invading empire and the way of Jesus colliding with the way of Caesar.

The kingdom of celebration was growing like mustard seed and taking root in the empire of entertainment through the lives of the earliest followers of Jesus of Nazareth. God's children were the mustard seed. Wherever they went, wherever they were thrown and landed—often through persecution—that's where the kingdom of God started moving out, moving in, and taking ground. It was an invasion of calm into chaos, restoration into ruin, repair into marring, and healing into brokenness.

To understand the vast difference between kingdom and empire and just how different the followers of Jesus were compared to the Greco-Roman world around them, look no further than the two kings who reigned during the time period recorded in the four gospels—Jesus and TIBERIUS.

When Jesus was born, Caesar AUGUSTUS was the emperor of Rome. He ruled from 27 BC–AD 14.[4]

During Jesus's earthly ministry, Tiberius Caesar was the emperor; he ruled from AD 14–AD 37.[5]

I often refer to this as "a tale of two kings."

Tiberius was the second emperor in the history of the Roman Empire.

History tells us that Tiberius was a reluctant ruler who never really wanted to be the emperor of the Roman Empire. After becoming emperor, he left Rome and moved into a spacious villa called Villa Jovis on top of the Isle of Capri. He left the Praetorian prefect L. Aelius Sejanus in charge back in Rome. Sejanus was ruthless, cunning, tyrannical, unpredictable, and hungry for power. The people feared Sejanus and despised Tiberius, seeing him as a deserter for leaving Rome.

At Villa Jovis on the Isle of Capri, the Roman historian SUETONIUS tells us that Tiberius engaged in vile and perverse behavior—debauchery and multi-faceted sexual perversions, including pedophilia. Tiberius wasted his days away in lavish hedonism, full of endless exploits intended only for his own personal gratification and satisfaction. He lived up to the famous line from the ancient Greek philosopher Protagoras, "Man is the measure of all things."[7]

The Roman historian Suetonius tells the story of Tiberius in a book called *The Lives of the Twelve Caesars*. In fact, Suetonius documents the stories of the first twelve emperors of the Roman Empire beginning with Caesar Augustus. These emperors would have reigned from the first-century AD to the early second-century AD. To put it into our biblical timeline, they were in power during Jesus's earthly ministry, Paul's ministry, and Peter's. They were the Roman rulers as the gospel started moving on the ground from Jerusalem to Judea and Samaria. It continued moving into the realms of these emperors and their empire.[6]

Taking on the Power of Jesus   47

When I take teams to Italy, we ferry out to the Isle of Capri, and we hike up to the modern ruins of Villa Jovis. We are hot, tired, and sweaty by the time we get to the top, but the view is absolutely breathtaking. It's immediately evident why this place was the perfect getaway location for a man as powerful as Caesar of Rome in the first-century AD.

We sit in the ruins of Villa Jovis, overlooking the gorgeous waters of the Gulf of Naples and the Gulf of Salerno, and study the Bible in the shade. We imagine Tiberius living out the way of empire and entertainment on that island, in that villa at the same time Jesus was walking around the Galilee, preaching the kingdom of God.

Tiberius embodied the way of empire in every way.

Jesus perfectly embodied the way of the kingdom in every way.

So while Tiberius was morally bankrupting himself and others at Villa Jovis, what was Jesus doing? During Tiberius's time as emperor, Jesus emerged from His Jordan River baptism and forty days in the wilderness as a Rabbi of the Galilee.

Read the following passage and underline every phrase that describes an action Jesus took.

Jesus went throughout Galilee, teaching in their synagogues, proclaiming the good news of the kingdom, and healing every disease and sickness among the people. News about him spread all over Syria, and people brought to him all who were ill with various diseases, those suffering severe pain, the demon-possessed, those

having seizures, and the paralyzed; and he healed them. Large crowds from Galilee, the Decapolis, Jerusalem, Judea and the region across the Jordan followed him.
MATTHEW 4:23-25

What word or phrase would you use to describe Tiberius Caesar's life, and what word or phrase would you use to describe Jesus's life?

Take a moment to reflect on your heart, mind, and actions as of late. What word or phrase would you use to describe yourself right now?

If you see room for growth, what word or phrase would you like to accurately describe you one day?

We immediately see the difference between empire and kingdom. Jesus did not use His power for Himself. He leveraged it on behalf of others. The church would learn and live this kingdom ethic so powerfully. They would leverage all they were and had for the sake of others.

> RATHER THAN SETTING UP A THRONE FROM WHICH TO RULE, JESUS WALKED AROUND THE GALILEE, SEEKING OUT THE LOST, BROKEN, SICK, AND DEMON-POSSESSED—THOSE STRUGGLING WITH THE TOILS OF LIFE.

Rather than setting up a throne from which to rule, Jesus walked around the Galilee, seeking out the lost, broken, sick, demon-possessed—those struggling with the toils of life. He was fully present with and among them, unafraid to enter into their pain, their stories, their hurt and maladies. Life was hard, and Jesus knew it. He started proclaiming the "good news of the kingdom" (Matt. 4:23).

A *shalomic* kingdom was coming into a world of empire, and it was good news indeed. The Jewish people were suffering under the heavy hand of Rome. Tiberius had power, but he had no character. He leveraged his power solely for himself. Jesus did not sit on any human throne, yet He demonstrated power and authority over sickness, brokenness, evil, and pain.

The kingdom of God would be subversive to the way of empire. No one living in the first-century AD would have ever imagined that a Jewish rabbi in some region far away from Rome would actually be more powerful than the Caesar of Rome. No one would have ever thought the kingdom Jesus was preaching about would still be here two thousand years later while the Roman Empire no longer stands.

The gospel on the ground was a beautiful first fruit of the great and holy overthrow that was underway.

Kingdom would undermine empire. Light would indeed invade the darkness. Darkness would indeed give way to light. Ruin would experience restoration. Weariness would give way to renewal. Dead things would be resurrected. Old and tired things would experience newness of life. Chaos would come to know calm.

I can't say it any better than C. S. Lewis did:

> Enemy-occupied territory—that is what this world is. Christianity is the story of how the rightful king has landed, you might say landed in disguise, and is calling us to take part in a great campaign of sabotage.[8]

It may seem strange, but I love sitting right in the ruins of Villa Jovis on the Isle of Capri with teams. I love every minute of it because it's an opportunity to participate in the great campaign of sabotage. As modern-day followers of Jesus, we sit in a place where so much evil happened—and redeem it.

We sit in the ruins of Villa Jovis, studying the Bible and imagining these two kings on the earth at the same time. When we finish studying, we sing. We sing hymns and worship songs to the living God. It's our way of shining light in a historically dark place. We bring the light in Word, prayer, and song. Space once used for utter debauchery is now space used to worship the living God.

The great sabotage is still underway, and you and I are actively participating in it every day.

> **Is there a place you think God is calling you to bring light? Something you see that needs to be redeemed? Journal your thoughts about what God might be asking you to stand in the way of.**

_____

_____

_____

_____

_____

_____

_____

_____

_____

session two **learn**

* Sketch of Solomon's temple

FILLED WITH THE FULLNESS OF GOD

READ PSALM 81.

Then write verse 10 in the space below.

When I first studied in Israel, I learned that the Jewish people trace certain rhythms of walking and participating with the living God throughout the story of the Bible. Participating in what? The restoration of all things. The Lord is making all things new, and we are part of that restorative work alongside Him in the earth.

According to the Jewish tradition, here's one of those rhythms:

We create space, and the living God fills it.

This goes all the way back to creation—literally, back to the genesis of the story. During creation, the living God started by creating space and then separating light from dark, land from air and from sea. After creating space, He began filling it with birds, animals, trees, vegetation, and eventually humans.

When the Jewish people went into the wilderness after the exodus, the Lord commanded them to build a tent for Him in their midst. He wanted to live among

52   THE GOSPEL ON THE GROUND

them during the wilderness years. They lived in tents, so would He. The tent was called the "tabernacle" or *mishkan* (meaning *dwelling*) in Hebrew.[9]

Once they built it, the glory of the Lord filled it.

Later, during the time of the Israelite monarchy, Solomon built a permanent house for the living God in Jerusalem. Solomon spent seven years building the Lord's house. When he finished building it, the glory of the Lord filled it.

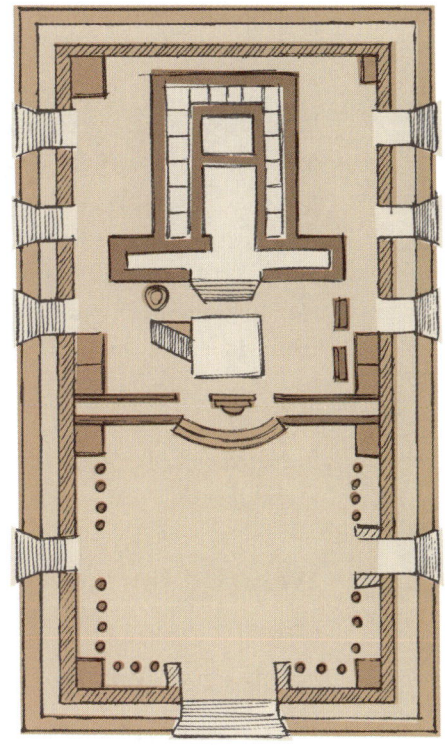

Empire—the way of the world—is marked by striving and straining. It's the way of an orphan who scrounges for sustenance. It's the way of trying to figure everything out, plotting your own life's path, and living or dying by your own wisdom as you choose your own way.

Kingdom is anchored in sonship and daughtership, practicing faithful trust in the living God to lead, guide, and provide. It's the way of posturing ourselves to receive from the Lord. It's a life of being shepherded, led, sustained in *shalom*, and "fed with the finest of wheat" as Psalm 81:16 says.

We create space.

The living God fills it.

We create space in our lives today by cultivating silence and practicing solitude. We also create space for God to fill every time we set our tables, every time we go to church together, every time we have people around our firepit, every time we throw a party, when we walk together, when we attend a wedding, or even go to a funeral.

It takes intentionality to put ourselves in God's way, to not let our hearts and our calendars be so busy and harried that we don't have space for emptiness that helps us come to terms with our need for God, to choose dependence on Him and a partnership with Him. We are purposeful to listen to God, to invite His provision and leadership and love into our lives. And we experience the gift of not having to figure it out on our own. We experience the gift of God's care and presence with us in our everyday lives—in the stillness of quiet moments where we hear from Him in His Word and in the moments of community where we feel His love and guidance in the family of faith.

In my life, I seek to create space for the living God to fill in a daily early morning walk with my dog Chester. It is like Groundhog Day at my house. We begin every morning in exactly the same way.

We wake up around 5:00 a.m., make the morning coffee, and head out on a long walk. No phone or earbuds. No music, no podcast, or sermon. We walk out my front door into the nothingness of the morning. My firstfruits given to God. It's just Him, Chester, and me walking. In silence.

Sometimes I pray. I often listen. In that nothingness, the Lord presents Himself. He walks with me.

> We are silent at the beginning of the day because God should have the first word, and we are silent before going to sleep because the last word also belongs to God.[10]

DIETRICH BONHOEFFER

I cannot explain it, but I inherit my best ideas on these walks. A kingdom calm is worked into my soul on these early morning walks. I somehow discern the ways I am meant to participate in the restoration of all things with the Lord. Someone will come to my mind, and I will call them later that day. I usually inherit the very things I'm writing about in this study during those early morning walks. They find me. I feel sabbathed after my morning walks. In walking with Him, I am reminded that He is doing the work. He is actively repairing the world. And I'm overjoyed that I get to join Him in it.

He changes us as we spend time in His presence. And He quiets our souls.

Above all, trust in the slow work of God. We are quite naturally impatient in everything to reach the end without delay. We should like to skip the intermediate stages. . . . Give Our Lord the benefit of believing that his hand is leading you.[11]

PIERRE TEILHARD DE CHARDIN

Somehow, this ancient practice rings very true in my life. On my walks, I open wide my mouth. The living God fills it. I get home from my walks postured to live into my day and into the world around me with a renewed mind and restored heart.

> **Do you have any rhythms in your life that prioritize time with God? If yes, what are they? If no, do you have any ideas of a rhythm you might want to try? Where can you make space to commune with God?**

session two **live**

LIVING OUT THE "GREAT SABOTAGE"

Well-behaved women seldom make history.[12]

LAUREL THATCHER ULRICH

✳ Street of Jerusalem: The Old City

Speaking of my early morning walks, one morning I was walking and came across this bumper sticker lying on my walking path.

I guess it had fallen off of someone's car or notebook as they drove or walked along. It had tape on the edges. It belonged somewhere else, but it landed on my walking path. I smiled as I bent down to pick it up. It almost felt like this bumper sticker was waiting for me, like it had something to say to me on that particular morning at that particular moment in my own life and journey.

I kept it. It's sitting beside me as I write this right now. It meant something to me.

You see, women were meaningfully present at Pentecost. When you think of the birth of the church, I want you to know that women have been an important part of this story of the church from the very beginning.

When witnesses at Pentecost asked Peter what in the world was happening when the Holy Spirit descended on the followers of Jesus, he quoted an Old Testament prophecy to explain the situation. The people asked if Jesus's followers were drunk. Peter replied,

> No, this is what was spoken by the prophet Joel:
> "'In the last days, God says,
> I will pour out my Spirit on all people.

> Your sons and DAUGHTERS will prophesy,
> your young men will see visions,
> your old men will dream dreams.
> Even on my servants, BOTH MEN AND WOMEN,
> I will pour out my Spirit in those days,
> and they will prophesy.'"
> ACTS 2:16-18, EMPHASIS MINE

Today as I write this, it's May 23, 2021, and it's Pentecost Sunday. Pentecost Sunday is marked on the annual church calendar and celebrated on the fiftieth day after Easter Sunday each year. It calls to mind the descent of the Holy Spirit upon the followers of Jesus while they were celebrating Pentecost (Shavuot) in Jerusalem some two thousand years ago, that specific milestone in the gospel spreading on the ground, in God's kingdom coming down to earth.

As we read earlier, C. S. Lewis called it a "great sabotage."[12] And Jesus said the kingdom of God is like a mustard seed.

As women who follow the way of Jesus, who are part of the kingdom of celebration invading the empire of entertainment in our own generation, this bumper sticker is a good reminder for all of us. We have a seat at this table. We each have a part to play. The living God is actively inviting us to partner with Him in the restoration, renewal, and repair of the world. Faithful women have gone before us. It's our turn.

We matter.

You matter.

The book of Acts and the formation of the early church is not just a story. It's not just their story. It's *our* story. This story is still going. It's still happening, and it's happening through you and me. Right now. Today.

I think of my friends who not only live for Jesus but also contend for the way of Jesus on the earth. They are serving, working, giving their lives away in prisons, orphanages, schools, churches, foster care and adoption, anti-trafficking organizations, hospitals, businesses, backyards, living rooms, and dinner tables.

They are bringing the kingdom of God to the earth as it is in heaven. Kingdom is invading empire through their lives, love, work, and service. *Shalom* is crashing into chaos. These women will bake you a cake and make a gospel ruckus all at once. They are not well-behaved in the world's way, but they are well-behaved in the subversive way of God's kingdom. They are very much like that mustard seed Jesus described.

As we move through this seven-session feast and journey together, understand that the book of Acts is *not* a history lesson. It's a living, breathing right-now story that pulses through our veins.

I pray we will be women who are *not* well-behaved in the way of the world. I pray, even as I'm writing on this Pentecost Sunday 2021, that we will be gospel-gorgeous in how we advance the kingdom of God on the earth.

How are you currently participating in the "great sabotage"?

What is the biggest thing that seems to hinder you from fully entering into the kingdom adventure?

In what ways would you like to participate in the "great sabotage"?

Where is God inviting you to partner with Him in the restoration, renewal, and repair of the world?

Who are the women in your life who are contending for the way of Jesus and the kingdom of God on the earth? Take time this week to reach out and encourage them, thanking them for their lives, witness, and example.

✷Temple of Hadrian in Ephesus

Kingdom of *Celebration* & Empire of *Entertainment*

MEANING INVADES MEANINGLESSNESS

SESSION THREE

Last week we learned about the birth of the church at Pentecost in Acts 2. The earliest followers of Jesus carried the teachings of Jesus. Now, they would travel carrying the flame of the Holy Spirit as well. Through these women and men, the words and works of Jesus would be put on display to the watching pagan world. The restoration, renewal, and repair of the world were underway. At Pentecost, three thousand were saved and baptized—and that was just the beginning.

Our storyline picks up briefly this week in Acts 3 and lives forward. The church was "scattered." Jesus's followers were first thrown like seed in Acts 7–8 after the stoning of Stephen. Stephen was the first martyr in the history of the church, but he would not be the last.

The people of the early church were thrown like a certain kind of seed: mustard seed. Everywhere they landed in Judea, Samaria, and throughout the Greco-Roman world, the kingdom of God started moving out and expanding the rule and reign of God in a world that was ruled by Caesar according to earthly standards.

As the gospel moved on the ground, God's kingdom of celebration started impacting and transforming Caesar's empire of entertainment. One life at a time. One day at a time. One city at a time. But what exactly does this mean? What is the kingdom of celebration? What is the empire of entertainment? What did it look like for a people of celebration to move so simply yet powerfully among the people of entertainment?

Today we will answer these questions through snapshots in the book of Acts and early church history. This gospel-gorgeous story continues.

Before we begin, let's pause for a simple reminder that we pull our chairs up to this biblical table to be transformed. We worship God through our desire to learn the story of the church so we can live with renewed purpose as the gospel moves on the ground through us today. We are now part of the kingdom of celebration living in an empire of entertainment. We are now making the way of Jesus known in a world of "Caesars." Rabbi Abraham Joshua Heschel said, "THE GREEKS LEARNED IN ORDER TO COMPREHEND. THE HEBREWS LEARNED IN ORDER TO REVERE. THE MODERN MAN LEARNS IN ORDER TO USE."[1]

We will travel the pages of the Bible together. We will welcome the adventure that is upon us, to live it out—together. So in our own way, we are a caravan.

*The Roman Colosseum was capable of holding fifty thousand spectators.

As we begin our biblical feast, before you watch the video teaching, take a few moments to answer the following questions:

What have you been pondering since last week's feast?

Four hundred years passed between the events recorded in Malachi (last book of the Old Testament) and Matthew (first book of the New Testament); this time frame is known as the Intertestamental Period. It represents that little blank, white page in your Bible between Malachi and Matthew. That white page is tricky because a lot happened during that four hundred years.

When you think of this time period between the Old and New Testaments, what do you think was happening?

When you hear the phrase "kingdom of celebration," what comes to your mind?

When you hear the phrase "empire of entertainment," what comes to your mind?

How have you lived like a mustard seed, spreading the kingdom of God, this past week?

Have you seen the Lord bring restoration, renewal, and repair to anything or anyone this past week? If so, explain.

Kingdom of Celebration & Empire of Entertainment

Watch
SESSION THREE

#GospelOnTheGround

THE FEAST

Use the following notes and space provided during our feast-teaching time. Feel free to add your own notes as you watch.

Jesus spent the vast majority of His life within a one-hundred-mile radius of where He was born. Yet His name is spoken and known in every corner of the earth. This is the story of how it happened—and is still happening.

The empire of entertainment is about scarcity and acquisition. The kingdom of God is anchored in Sabbath rest.

The Intertestamental Period is the four hundred years between the books of Malachi and Matthew.

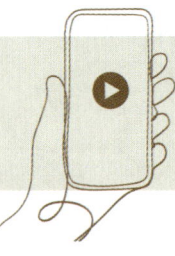

TO ACCESS THE VIDEO TEACHING SESSIONS,
USE THE INSTRUCTIONS IN THE BACK OF YOUR BIBLE STUDY BOOK.

Hellenism is an emphasis on individualism, education, wealth, and competition (sport).

The greatest example of the kingdom of entertainment was the Colosseum in Rome.

One of the greatest examples of the kingdom being like a mustard seed is the story of Telemachus.

Jesus taught that the Messiah would not only come once, but He would come again. There would be two visitations.

session three **discuss**

LET'S YESHIVA!

As we make our way through some of the book of Acts with early church histories told alongside it, let's take some time to *yeshiva* together. Processing with your Christian community is a healthy, vibrant pathway to apply what we are learning.

We do not simply want to know these stories in the Bible; we want to enter into the story of God and live it out in our own day and time. The gospel is still moving on the ground. The kingdom of celebration is still transforming the empire of entertainment, and we are partnering with the Lord in the restoration, renewal, and repair of the world.

Take some time to discuss the following questions with your group.

What one thing that you learned today do you want to share with others this week?

When you see how the Lord used Telemachus to bring the Colosseum entertainment enterprise to its knees, does it make you wonder what God wants to do through your life? Do you have any ideas about what He might want to do?

You are living in the year of the Lord's favor today. What are some of the ways you are experiencing the Lord's favor in your life right now? What are some ways you are seeing the favor of the Lord in your family and friends' lives right now?

LIVING FORWARD FROM PENTECOST

Every single follower of Jesus who experienced the miraculous gift of the Holy Spirit at Pentecost woke up the next morning and went to work. A mundane Monday followed the extraordinary events of Pentecost. Followers of Jesus went right back to their lives, their families, their jobs, and their communities.

I wonder how they felt when they woke up the next morning. Often the morning after something incredible can feel a bit sad, lonely, and even empty. Everything probably seemed the same, but nothing would ever be exactly the same. They would never be the same. The world would never be the same. They now carried the flame of the Spirit, the divine enablement to not only teach what Jesus taught but to do what He did.

You might recall from Session One that we learned the importance of the rabbi-*talmid* relationship in Jesus's first-century Jewish world. When you follow a rabbi, you don't want to just know what he knows. You want to be just like him. You want to do what he does.

Acts 2 is immediately followed by Acts 3, and this incredible story gives us a snapshot of what the rest of the book of Acts will be like after Pentecost.

READ ACTS 3:1-10.

Acts 3:1-10 serves almost like a movie trailer for the coming feature-length film of Acts. You read this story, and you know the book of Acts is about to be action-packed and gospel-gorgeous as the followers of Jesus started living forward from Pentecost.

> **THEY NOW CARRIED THE FLAME OF THE SPIRIT, THE DIVINE ENABLEMENT TO NOT ONLY TEACH WHAT JESUS TAUGHT, BUT TO DO WHAT HE DID.**

What three men are described in this account (vv. 1-2)?

What do we know about the man that Peter and John encountered at the temple? What description are we given when Peter and John first meet him (v. 2-3)?

What information are we given about him when he left his interaction with Peter and John (vv. 7-8)?

What effect did this man's transformation have on the community around him (vv. 9-10)?

In Acts 3, Peter and John were going to the temple at 3:00 p.m. Last session we learned why. The daily sacrifices, the *tamid* sacrifices, were offered at 9:00 a.m. and 3:00 p.m., so we imagine Peter and John were headed to the temple for the afternoon sacrifice. As they entered the Gate Beautiful, they encountered a man lame from birth. At that moment, they carried not only the teachings of Jesus but the flame, the indwelling of the Holy Spirit, and in the name of Jesus, this man was made well. It was almost like a tremor of the coming church age—the words and works of Jesus active in the embodied lives of Jesus's followers.

They would not only know what Jesus had taught them, but they would do the very things they watched Him do during His earthly ministry.

I have always loved how Peter and John didn't see this moment coming in this story. The moment found them. They were just being faithful in their day, doing the next right thing along the way. For Jews in Jerusalem, 3:00 p.m. was approaching, and it was an opportunity to go pray at God's house with others. They were minding their own business. They were simply on their way to pray, but the Lord had so much more planned. A whole lot more than praying was about to happen.

They didn't plan it. Not only did they not plan it, but there's no indication in the passage that they were even looking for anything incredible to happen.

This story would repeat itself in so many ways throughout the book of Acts and the New Testament. The kingdom of God started moving out with great impact in Jerusalem. As the words and works of Jesus were made known through the followers of Jesus, more and more believed and were added to their number. The kingdom was indeed growing like a mustard seed. Just two chapters later in Acts 5:12-16, we find this beautiful and powerful movement:

> The apostles performed many signs and wonders among the people. And all the believers used to meet together in Solomon's Colonnade. No one else dared join them, even though they were highly regarded by the people. Nevertheless, more and more men and women believed in the Lord and were added to their number. As a result, people brought the sick into the streets and laid them on beds and mats so that at least Peter's shadow might fall on some of them as he passed by. Crowds gathered also from the towns around Jerusalem, bringing their sick and those tormented by impure spirits, and all of them were healed.

NOW READ MATTHEW 4:23-25 AND COMPLETE THE CHART.

	Matthew 4:23-25	Acts 5:12-16
Who is doing the work in this passage?		
Describe what's happening in this passage.		

Do you notice any similarities between the two accounts? Explain.

Here again, we see great parallels between the work of Jesus and the work of His followers on the earth. As the followers of Jesus went about their lives, opportunities for the words and works of Jesus to live through them met them on the journey. The gospel started moving along the ground from Jerusalem to Judea, Samaria, and right into the heart of the Roman Empire.

There is much for us to learn from this first "snapshot," this movie trailer for the book of Acts. The Christian life is lived "as we go." We don't have to plan for kingdom adventures. They find us. We live with the simple *shalom* of seeking to do the next right thing. We rarely see it coming before the Lord shows up in some incredible way in our lives. We can trust that the kingdom adventures will come along the way.

When was the last time you walked into a kingdom moment you did not see coming? Explain what happened.

What kingdom adventures have been finding you lately? Where do you feel you are being invited to partner with the living God in the restoration, renewal, and repair of the world?

What tends to make you shrink back from the kingdom adventures that come your way?

What would you need to overcome?

session three **look**

A TALE OF TWO CITIES: NAZARETH AND SEPPHORIS

✳ View from Mount Precipice overlooking present day Nazareth

Jesus spent the vast majority of His life within a one-hundred-mile radius from where He was born. He was born in Bethlehem in Judea. He grew up in Nazareth in the Galilee. And He would go on to live in Capernaum, a coastal town right on the Sea of Galilee (Matt. 4:12-13).

In the first century, Nazareth was a small Jewish village. We would not even think of it as a city or even a town. Jesus grew up with Joseph, Mary, and His brothers and sisters in a tiny dot on a big map of the world.

So many of the events and stories in the book of Acts and the rest of the New Testament happened well outside of the borders of Israel. The earliest followers of Jesus were "scattered" (*diaspora*) like mustard seed throughout the Roman Empire. The gospel would reach places like EPHESUS, Philippi, Corinth, Thessalonica, and ultimately Rome itself. The followers of Jesus would make kingdom impact in the world of empire. They would teach others and live out the way of Jesus in cities with temples, theaters, hippodromes, brothels, bath houses, and arenas.

These cities could not have been more different from Jewish villages, towns, or even the city of Jerusalem itself. Did Jesus have any understanding of this world that His followers would be thrust into after His ascension back into heaven? Did He have any sense of what they would see, what they would face, and what they would experience as followers of Jesus in the world of Caesar?

Kingdom of Celebration & Empire of Entertainment

A map of the Galilee in the first-century AD sheds incredible light on these questions. Nazareth was a tiny, insignificant place in the Mediterranean world. However, just four miles away stood a large and impressive Greco-Roman city called Sepphoris. Located on top of a hill, its Hebrew name was *Zippori* meaning *bird*, and it overlooked Jewish villages like Nazareth and Cana.[2] It was a large Greek and Roman city on a hill.

Jesus grew up in the shadows of Sepphoris.

But as a Jew, would He have ever gone to Sepphoris?

JOSEPHUS, a Jewish priest, scholar, and historian, called Sepphoris the "Jewel of Galilee."[3] It was conveniently located along two major highways, the Via Maris and Acre-Tiberias. The bustling city of Sepphoris would have been a major hub, employing people from all over the Galilee.

READ MATTHEW 13:55.

What does this passage tell us about Joseph?

Joseph, Jesus's earthly father, was a "carpenter" (Matt. 13:55; Mark 6:3). The Greek word for *carpenter* is *tekton* meaning *builder*.[4] Historical records tell us that stone, not wood, was the primary building material of the Galilee region in the first century.[5]

We envision Joseph as more of a stoneworker or a stonemason. Traditionally Jewish fathers apprenticed their sons in the family trade starting at age twelve or so. Jesus would have learned to be a *tekton* like His father, most likely learning to build with stone. In other words, Jesus knows how to swing a hammer.

THE GOSPEL ON THE GROUND

We can easily imagine Joseph and Jesus waking up every morning during the week and walking the four miles from Nazareth to Sepphoris to work as *tektons*, building this great city in the Galilee region.

When I take teams to Israel, we visit the magnificent ruins of Sepphoris. It is sometimes called "Mosaic City" because some of the best mosaics in all of Israel are found in Sepphoris.[6] More than forty mosaic floors depict a vibrant and bustling Roman life and culture there. There's a famous mosaic of a Roman woman in the Dionysus House; she is called the "Mona Lisa of the Galilee." As you can see, it is stunningly beautiful to this day.

One of the most impressive features of ancient Sepphoris was a large theater built into the eastern side of the hill. It held over four thousand people. Sepphoris was part of the empire of entertainment. This theater would have hosted Greek and Roman plays and concerts, among other things. When the teams and I are at Sepphoris, we sit in the ancient ruins of this theater. And we consider:

What if Joseph and Jesus helped build it?

What if some of the stones we're sitting on were actually laid by the Son of God Himself?

If so, Jesus would have been exposed to Greek and Roman theater with its "hypocrites" as the actors in those days. Jesus used this term "hypocrite" several times in Matthew 23 when confronting the teachers of the law and Pharisees of His day. Over and over we read this line from Jesus, "Woe to you, teachers of the law and Pharisees, you hypocrites!" Jesus was saying that the Pharisees and the teachers of the day were acting and not being genuine. They were playing a part, like an actor, rather than genuinely shepherding and caring for the Jewish people. He could have been comparing them to the actors He had seen in the theater at Sepphoris.

Jesus was a Jewish boy growing up in Nazareth. Nazareth was part of the kingdom of celebration. He would have attended synagogue, pondered and discussed Torah with His family and community, prayed the *Shema* a few times a day, and watched His mother Mary light the two *Shabbat* candles at sundown on Friday night, welcoming the Sabbath into their home like a bride. He would have traveled in a community caravan to Jerusalem for the festivals of Passover, Shavuot (Pentecost), and Tabernacles.

And Jesus grew up four miles from the empire of entertainment. We imagine Jesus being exposed to Greek and Roman culture if He took work trips to Sepphoris with His father. He would have seen the world He came to save. He would have seen the brothels, the bathhouses, the temples to pagan gods, and the AGORAS (shopping malls) with their goods from all over the empire.

He would have seen the darkness.

He would have felt the lostness, the striving and straining of a world in need of God.

He would have seen the chaos, the brokenness, the way people used and abused one another for the sake of personal pleasure or gain.

He would have seen the emptiness of the empire of entertainment.

He would have seen a world that desperately needed the kingdom of salvation, restoration, renewal, and repair.

And Jesus would have known exactly the world into which His disciples were going to be thrown, like mustard seed. With eyes wide open, He would have learned firsthand what the gospel moving on the ground to "the ends of the earth" would mean for His earliest followers.

Who knows, Jesus could have been referencing Sepphoris when He said to His disciples,

> You are the light of the world. A town built on a hill cannot be hidden. Neither do people light alamp and put it under a bowl. Instead they put it on its stand, and it gives light to everyone in the house. In the same way, let your light shine before others, that they may see your good deeds and glorify your Father in heaven.
> **MATTHEW 5:14-16**

session three **learn**

* Roman theater of Sepphoris

A TABLE OF WELCOME

The kingdom of celebration is still moving into the empire of entertainment today. And it's moving through you and me. One of the simplest and yet most profound ways we can participate in the kingdom of celebration is through table fellowship.

Eating together is kingdom-of-God business and celebrations are almost always accompanied with food.

Birthdays.

Weddings.

Anniversaries.

Graduations.

Baby showers.

End-of-school-year parties.

One of the most valuable kingdom-of-God things you own is your dinner table. It's where you set a table to join together in food, fellowship, harmony, and affiliation with others. The table gathers us together. It summons us to a moment, a moment of sharing. Stories are shared around the table. Our stories. Their stories. Hearts are shared around the table. Problems and prayer requests are shared around the table. Solutions and prayers happen around the table.

There's something very comforting about eating with people. Our dinner tables are a strategic ministry outpost for the kingdom of God. Eating together was one of the highest values in the ancient Jewish world and still is today throughout the Middle East. Whom you ate with said everything about you—it was your affiliation with them. Whom you ate with symbolized whom you welcomed, embraced, and accepted.

> The Son of Man came eating and drinking, and they say, "Here is a glutton and a drunkard, a friend of tax collectors and sinners."
> MATTHEW 11:19a

Jesus loved table fellowship. He was known for it. He leads this kingdom of celebration.

READ JOHN 2:1-11.

Speaking of celebration, what did Jesus do at this wedding?

Does the Bible give us any noteworthy information about this miracle (you know, apart from the miracle) (v. 11)?

It is so fitting that Jesus's first public miracle was changing water to wine at a wedding. At a celebration. And in changing the water to wine, He ensured that the party would continue. The celebration would continue. The table fellowship would continue. The welcoming, embracing, and accepting would continue.

In the Gospel of Luke, Jesus was often on His way to a meal, at a meal, or leaving a meal. It seems Jesus loves food and He loves eating with people. Jesus did not come with a sword to usher in the kingdom of God. He set tables. A lot of them. Often.

In Matthew 11, as we read earlier, Jesus said that people were calling Him a "glutton and a drunkard, a friend of tax collectors and sinners." Jesus met with people at tables. He talked with people at tables. He told stories at tables. He ate with people often. He was showing the world what the living God's table of welcome looked like. No matter who or what you were, you had a seat at Jesus's table. He offers the same invitation to us today.

Table fellowship was a way to participate in and celebrate the restoration, renewal, and repair of the world. It still is.

You and I live between the two visitations, or comings, of Jesus. We are living in the *ratzon l'adonai*—the year of the Lord's favor.[7,8] I love this beautiful truth. One of the most important ways we can participate in and celebrate the Lord's favor is through our own table fellowship practices with family, friends, neighbors, and community.

✴ Kristi's dining table

What does your dining table look like?

What is it made of?

What is currently sitting on your dining table?

What usually happens at your dining table?

Who eats at your table?

Whom would you like to invite to eat at your table?

Whom do you know who is hurting and needs to be comforted at your table?

Whom do you know who is fearful and needs to be encouraged at your table?

Whom do you know who is lost and needs to be invited to come home to God at your table?

Whom do you know who is lonely and needs to find meaningful conversation at your table?

The living God has a table, a "table of welcome." He is inviting the whole world to come to His table. He is inviting them through you and me. Your table is a foretaste of His great banquet table.

Set your table this week. Invite people to it. Join in the kingdom of celebration with good food, great conversation, and lots of laughter.

Eat and fellowship like you are living in the year of the Lord's favor.

session three **live**

* Nazareth today

FOR, NOT AGAINST

Watch out for the Christian who spends more time telling you what she is against rather than what she is for.

READ ACTS 5:12-16.

We read this passage earlier this week but try to consider it with fresh eyes.

What about this passage resonates with you most and why?

After reading this passage, what would you say the early church was for?

The earliest followers of Jesus lived for, not against. They sought to bring the kingdom of God to earth as it is in heaven. They wanted to create, to build, to share, to bless, to encourage, to meet needs, to make a positive impact, and to make a difference in the darkness of the world of empire. Rather than running from this darkness, they inhabited it and announced the year of the Lord's favor in it, both in word and deed.

In other words, they were for the kingdom of God, not so much against the Roman Empire. It's hard to minister to someone or something when you feel against them. If the world feels adversarial to you, you will tend to avoid it, judge it, and lack empathy for the people living in darkness.

Kingdom of Celebration & Empire of Entertainment

But if you see the world of empire as a space that needs the light you can bring, as an opportunity to usher in the kingdom of celebration and bring meaning to meaninglessness, you will engage and lean in wholeheartedly like the believers we read about in the book of Acts and in the early church histories.

Being against something is passive. You can sit on your couch all day being against things. Being against something is easy.

But being for something is active. You have to get off of the couch and do something to help. Being for something will cost you, but it's worth it.

The book of Acts tells the story of the people of the kingdom of God who were for the coming kingdom, not passively against the Roman Empire. Rather than fighting darkness, they simply brought light. Rather than protesting hunger, they simply fed the poor. Rather than raging against sickness, they offered compassion and aid. They lived for the kingdom of God, not against the empire of entertainment.

They saw the brokenness, and they entered into it.

They saw the loneliness, and they invited people to join the family of God.

They saw the hunger, and they fed it.

They saw the emptiness of entertainment, and they offered a life of active, meaningful partnership with the living God.

They saw the sick, and they offered help and aid.

We see the gospel moving on the ground from Jerusalem to Judea, Samaria, "and to the ends of the earth" just as Jesus said in Acts 1:8.

In Acts 3, Peter and John healed a lame man in Jerusalem.

In Acts 8, Philip preached the good news, impure spirits came out of people, and the lame and paralyzed were healed in Samaria.

In Acts 19, Paul was doing extraordinary miracles, so much so that handkerchiefs and aprons that had touched Paul would heal illnesses and cast out evil spirits in Ephesus.

We read the book of Acts, and we see an invitation within it. We are invited to be part of the kingdom of God—known by what we are for rather than what we are against. As we close this week, take some time to ponder and answer the following questions.

What are you for?

Why do you have such a passion for those kingdom things?

Are you currently engaged in those kingdom things?

What obstacles are hindering you from engaging more fully?

Name one step you can take this week to engage, lean in, and participate in the gospel moving on the ground through your passion and the things you are for.

Kingdom of *Abundance* & Empire of *Scarcity*

SUBVERSIVE GENEROSITY ON THE MOVE

SESSION FOUR

Last week we learned about the empire of entertainment during the time chronicled in the book of Acts and the New Testament. The early church was thrown like mustard seed into this world, beginning in Acts 7–8 and beyond.

A world of meaninglessness was deeply disrupted and impacted by the kingdom of meaning. In the story of Telemachus, we learned just how potent and powerful one faithful life could be when lived out before the eyes of the Roman world. As we will see this week, Telemachus would not be the last to give his life as a martyr.

The Roman Empire had several "Vegas" cities full of theaters, amphitheaters, hippodromes, bathhouses, temples, and brothels. The earliest followers of Jesus who faced persecution and were scattered (*diaspora*) like mustard seed landed and took root in these cities. The kingdom of celebration started impacting and transforming these cities, these people, and their communities. Meaninglessness gave way to meaning.

We also learned that we are living in the *ratzon l'adonai*—the year of the Lord's favor. Even today, right now in this current moment, you and I are living in the twilight between the two visitations of Jesus, waiting for the sunrise of His second coming. Knowing His story in the Gospels empowers us and allows us to be hopeful as we look for Him to come again. Jesus behind us, with us now, and in front of us yet.

This week we will see the gospel well on its way, moving on the ground outside of Jerusalem, Judea, and Samaria. Even at the ends of the earth, many were bearing witness to the followers of Jesus, hearing and seeing them live out the way of Jesus.

We will learn about one ancient city in particular, a city called Antioch. It was in that city Christians were first called "Christian." (See Acts 11:26.) What were the followers of Jesus doing in Antioch that caused the pagan world to give them the name "Christian"? What could a small minority of people living in a thriving and bustling Greco-Roman city actually do to make the Roman world take notice? Although we still carry the name of "Christian" to this day, we will see that the name carried a very different meaning back then.

The kingdom of abundance started invading the empire of scarcity. This week, we will see how the earliest followers of Jesus lived like they could not lose. Rather than holding on, they let go. Rather than hunkering down and bracing themselves, they lived openly with a generosity that shocked the Greco-Roman world. Their adversaries could not do enough to them to make them stop and could not take enough from them to make them stingy.

The gospel-gorgeous story continues today.

Our snapshots through the book of Acts continue alongside early church histories. As always, we are reminded that this is not just their story—it's our story too. This story lives on today in you and me. The gospel is still moving on the ground. The kingdom is living and on the move. We are meant to be an active people, participating with the living God in the repair of the world.

As we begin our biblical feast, before you watch the video teaching, take a few moments to answer the following questions.

When you hear the phrase "kingdom of abundance," what comes to your mind?

When you hear the phrase "empire of scarcity," what comes to your mind?

What kinds of things do you think the early followers of Jesus were doing in ANTIOCH that earned them the name "Christian"?

How have you lived like a mustard seed, spreading the kingdom of God, this past week?

Have you seen the Lord bring restoration, renewal, and repair to anything or anyone this past week? Explain what you've seen.

Watch
SESSION FOUR

#GospelOnTheGround

THE FEAST
How can we blasphame with how faithful

Use the following notes and space provided during our feast-teaching time. Feel free to add your own notes as you watch.

Jesus spent the vast majority of His life within a one-hundred-mile radius of where He was born. Yet His name is spoken and known in every corner of the earth. This is the story of how it happened—and is still happening.

Legend holds that the flames would not consume Polycarp.

Look at how Polycarp treated those who came to his door

*Abundance v. scarcity
↳ we do not need to worry*

Christians were first called "Christian" in Antioch on the Orontes.

*Acts 11:19 Church in Antioch 16 Antioch's
Given by the paegen church
what were they doing?
Antoich - people went to lose themselves. Full of entertainment
↳ vegas*

TO ACCESS THE VIDEO TEACHING SESSIONS,
USE THE INSTRUCTIONS IN THE BACK OF YOUR BIBLE STUDY BOOK.

How do you think the roman citizens reacted?
- *Christians were arrested*
- *Property being confiscated*

They didn't try to stop death

Do people know I am a Christian

Am I conforming to the things of this world.

Christians were known as "heretics" in the Roman Empire.

Stand my ground → *hareses - taking or choosing a different way*

3 things they were doing:
1. Refuse to participate in the imperial cult
2. They were heretics   ↓ *Everyone has a chance*
3. Took human life seriously

Would I stand against? How do I do this well
Phillipians 1:21 - To live is Christ, to die is gain

Empire of scarcity: orphan, striving, straining, withholding   *we cannot lose*
Kingdom of abundance: son/daughter, Sabbathed, contentment, generous

* *Babies were left out to die*
* *Interesting how adoption was a big thing*
   ↳ *taking in those who have been put out*

Look at what came from all of this

We are a kingdom people actively participating with the living God in the redemption, restoration, renewal, and repair of the world.

Luke 24 eyes were opened

They just kept giving. We are never done
Giving looks so different
"eyes were opened" go back to genesis 3:6-7
It gave them hope   *Revelation 21*

As followers of Jesus, our eyes have been opened twice. We live in a world of people whose eyes have only been opened once. They need an invitation into a kingdom of celebration, meaning, and abundance.

Hope - the active conviction that despair will not have the final word

Hebrews 12:1-2

Kingdom of Abundance & Empire of Scarcity

session four **discuss**

LET'S YESHIVA!

Take some time to discuss the following questions with your group:

What one thing that you learned today do you want to share with others this week?

How do you tend to respond when you face great difficulty, trials, or tribulations?

If you could ask Polycarp one question, what would it be? Why?

Do you feel like your life is currently more anchored in the empire of scarcity or the kingdom of abundance?

If you could ask Mr. and Mrs. Cleopas one question, what would it be? Why?

As a person whose eyes have been opened twice, what are you seeing right now? What do you feel like the Lord is doing in your heart, family, community, and church?

Acts 1:8
"witness" — martyr ← greek word Marterian
- something is hard doesn't mean it's hard
Policart — means much fruit

Prayer requests:
Michelle - Nate's job - owes money
  her job search   getting a lawyer
Celeste - a heart of abundance
  ↳ with her job and comission
Sonni - make it through the week
  with work & Florida
  processing and not overthinking
Fatima - Little brother Daniel - verbally harassed by teacher
Aunt & her family - trying to have a baby
Praise - got promoted

session four **follow-up**

BROTHERS AND SISTERS

READ ACTS 2:42-47.

The generosity of the early church was striking—almost unnerving to us. We read these generosity stories throughout the book of Acts, and we wonder why they were so generous toward one another. They actually lived out the more modern-day motto, "Leave no man behind."

> THE EARLY CHURCH SAW THEMSELVES AS A FAMILY.

When we read the first few chapters of the book of Acts, we're reading about deep compassion in the context of Jerusalem. Early followers of Jesus were exhibiting kindness toward their own—local and neighborly generosity.

The early church saw themselves as a family, not as collective individuals with different last names who hung out from time to time. Jesus was the firstborn and the only begotten Son of God. They were adopted into this eternal family with a high and holy Father who promised to never leave them nor forsake them. They took seriously the truth that each of them had been saved and adopted into God's family. This made them siblings to one another—brothers and sisters in Christ. They would never be alone again, not in this life or the one to come. They loved and cared for one another as siblings in a family, not simply friends who shared a faith in God.

The first-century Jewish world was a communal culture and an honor/shame culture. Honor and shame were not just individual, they were communal values. This cultural marker was never about how just one person was doing. It was always about how everyone was doing. They lived every day in the "we" and not the "me."

The first two siblings in the story of the Bible are Cain and Abel. They give us the first glimpse of the sibling relationship. Many sibling relationships would follow—some of these names may sound familiar to you:

- Isaac and Ishmael

- Jacob and Esau

- Joseph and his brothers—Reuben, Simeon, Levi, Judah, Dan, Naphtali, Gad, Asher, Issachar, Zebulun, and Benjamin. (Plus one sister that we know of, Dinah.)

- Moses, Miriam, and Aaron

A profound question was asked and answered between the first two siblings, Cain and Abel. Cain killed his brother Abel while the two of them were in a field together (Gen. 4:8). After this, the Lord had an important and timeless conversation with Cain.

> Then the LORD said to Cain, "Where is your brother Abel?"
> "I don't know," he replied. "Am I my brother's keeper?"
> **GENESIS 4:9**

The rest of the Bible answers this question with a resounding yes! We are indeed our brother's keeper and are meant to live meaningfully and generously for the benefit and honor of the family, the group, and the community.

The ancient Israelites left the corners of their fields unharvested so the poor, widows, and orphans could have food to eat. The practice of jubilee ensured that debts would be paid so that siblings would not end up in lifelong debt and servitude to one another. The practice of the kinsman-redeemer that we see in the story of Boaz, Ruth, and Naomi was to ensure that the wives and children of men lost in war would not be left isolated, destitute, and without family, protection, or provision.

There's more to the Cain and Abel narrative to unpack here. Let's keep reading.

> The LORD said, "What have you done? Listen!
> Your brother's blood cries out to me from the ground."
> **GENESIS 4:10**

The word *blood* here is plural.[1] It is not just Abel's blood that was crying out to the Lord. It was the entire bloodline that would never be born because Cain snuffed out Abel's life. For the Jewish people, killing was a communal and generational act. It was never the loss of one life, but the loss of the generations that would never be born.

> If any man has caused a single life to perish from Israel, he is deemed by Scripture as if he had caused a whole world to perish; and anyone who saves a single soul from Israel, he is deemed by Scripture as if he had saved a whole world.[2]
>
> **MISHNAH SANHEDRIN 4:5**

We are our brother's keepers. We are siblings in the Lord. Caring for the family of God is one of the ways we participate with the living God in the restoration and renewal of the world, starting with our own families and faith communities.

What if our generosity not only helps the person but her entire lineage?

What if helping one person is like helping a world?

What if our lack of generosity not only harms the person but her entire lineage?

What if a lack of generosity not only harms the person but a world?

What if generosity is like a rock skipping along the water—the harder you throw it, the further it goes?

The earliest followers of Jesus lived with such extravagant generosity toward one another because they were living like they were their brother's keepers. It was the honorable thing to do. It was the right thing to do.

I think Acts 2:44-45 is one of the most convicting and challenging yet beautiful and buoyant passages in the entire New Testament. As you know, it reads:

> All the believers were together and had everything in common. They sold property and possessions to give to anyone who had need.

Extravagant generosity is *still* the right thing to do today. As followers of Jesus, we should be the most generous people in the entire world. We are not orphans left to ourselves. We are not fatherless. We are not without the family of God. We can afford to give our lives away knowing the living God will give them back to us in manifold ways. We are part of the kingdom of abundance in an empire of scarcity.

Let Jesus be our anthem and generosity be our theme.

What about the abundance of the early church is most challenging to you?

Do you find it hard to be generous with others? Explain.

Is it easier for you to be generous with the people closest to you or people you don't know well? Why?

Brainstorm a few ways that you might practice generosity. (It doesn't necessarily have to be financial generosity; you might give of your time or skills; you might give words of encouragement. Think outside of the box.)

SELFLESS LOVE IS ALWAYS COSTLY. FEAR CAN'T AFFORD IT, PRIDE DOESN'T UNDERSTAND IT, BUT FRIENDS NEVER FORGET IT.[3]

BOB GOFF

Take a moment to look back over the list you just wrote and pick one to try out this next week. (Tell your group how it goes; they'd love to know!)

session four **look**

GENEROUS WITNESS TO THE PAGAN WORLD

READ ACTS 4:32-37.

Jot down any parts of the Acts 4 passage that stick out to you.

Earlier this week, we read Acts 2:42-47, another passage that describes the openhearted nature of the early church. Do you notice any significant differences between the two passages? Record any insights you find.

The generosity that the earliest followers of Jesus practiced in Jerusalem became the generosity they showed to the greater Roman world.

It's one thing to be generous with your siblings. It's quite another to be generous with others—Gentiles, Greeks, and Romans. No matter how much the Roman Empire persecuted the church, she responded with faithful, generous resilience. You could not take enough from them to make them stop giving or caring for others.

By the time we come to Acts 4, the followers of Jesus were not only being generous, they were selling their possessions, their homes, and their land to make sure everyone in the community was cared for. Possessions. Houses. Land. I believe the extravagance of the generosity in Acts 4 shows that this money was for more than just the followers of Jesus. The early church was likely not a large group at this

Kingdom of Abundance & Empire of Scarcity

point, and it included people from other places who may have lacked the funds necessary to live in Jerusalem beyond their intended stay for the festival. What if this generosity included selling land and houses to provide for the needy around them or to allow the new followers to stay connected to one another? To show others the love and kindness of God?

This kind of generosity is something more than giving out of overflow. It is costly kindness lived out in a world of scarcity. One of the main ways the church served as witnesses (*martyres*) was through their charity.[4]

Why did the church need to be so generous with others and not just their own?

Historically, Christians were known as atheists and heretics throughout the empire. They were going against the norm; at that time, the norm was the imperial cult. The people of the Roman Empire worshiped its emperor. But the followers of Jesus worshiped Jesus alone. They were heretics because they had taken another way, the way of Jesus and not the way of Caesar.

Imagine a Gentile, Greek, or Roman living with family in the Roman Empire. Imagine he or she becomes a follower of Jesus, a Christian. How would the family respond to this news? How would a Roman family respond to one of their own becoming what was considered an atheist, a heretic, and an enemy of Rome?

In some cases, new believers would be kicked out of their families—abandoned and rejected. They would lose their biological families. This meant they also lost any sense of financial tethering, provision, or even vocational connections that would normally have come through their family's social network. Ostracized, considered an atheist and a heretic, they would be cast out and on their own. So perhaps the extravagance of the early church was an act of faith, to make provision for the Gentiles they believed God would bring into His family.

This sheds incredible insight into some seemingly strange and difficult words of Jesus given to us in Matthew 10:34-36. He said,

> Do not suppose that I have come to bring peace to the earth. I did not come to bring peace, but a sword. For I have come to turn "a man against his father, a daughter against her mother, a daughter-in-law against her mother-in-law—a man's enemies will be the members of his own household."

Jesus never preached violence or instructed His followers to abandon their families. He was saying that following Him was a divisive thing. The empire of darkness would respond when the kingdom of light showed up. Following Jesus would come with a price, sometimes a very hefty price tag indeed. Jesus didn't separate families, but following Him would divide families. Gentile followers of Jesus would have experienced this very pain in their world.

But the family of God would welcome, embrace, and accept them into their new spiritual family. They experienced a warm welcome into the kingdom way as they left the way of the world. And the family of God would also help provide for their physical and financial needs. These new Gentile believers were now siblings, adopted into the family of God through faith in Jesus.

Timothy Keller noted that while the Roman world was practicing sexual promiscuity, the followers of Jesus practiced financial promiscuity: "The early church was strikingly different from the culture around it in this way—the pagan society was stingy with its money and promiscuous with its body. A pagan gave nobody their money and practically gave everybody their body. And the Christians came along and gave practically nobody their body and they gave practically everybody their money."[5]

As the gospel moved along the ground, so often kingdom generosity fueled its spread in a world of scarcity. Unearned generosity will change a person's life.

Generosity is attractive. A generous person lives open-handed, not tight-fisted. Her life has a flow, a buoyancy that comes from a faithful trust in the living God to fund her life in every way. The early church could take Jesus at His word and lose their lives as witnesses (*martyres*) because they had faith that He would give their lives back to them.

I was privileged to have a mentor for twenty-five years. I met her in college, and she faithfully mentored me and many others until we lost her to cancer in the summer of 2018. I feel the loss of her so often. Many times when I am speaking or teaching, the words coming out of my mouth are things she taught me along the way. She made many deposits into my spiritual growth and maturity over the years. I am indebted to her forever and so grateful for her.

One of the things she taught me while I was in college has stayed with me to this very moment as I write. I have tried to live it and embody it. I have used it as a guide in moments of financial decision over the last twenty-five years. She would often say, "Kristi, seek to be the most generous person in the room."

The first time I heard it I did not get it. Really? Wouldn't I rather be the smartest? Fastest? Richest? Those were my thoughts as a young collegiate whippersnapper. A few times, I was brave enough to ask her just those questions.

She would say, "The kingdom doesn't need your smarts, agility, or riches. She has all the smarts, agility, and riches she needs. She needs someone to give it away to the world."

My mentor would have done well living in the days of the early church.

FABULOUS FABIOLA

The first hospital in Rome was founded by a woman named Fabiola in AD 394. Fabiola was a wealthy, free noblewoman in the empire. It would have been so easy for her to waste her life in the empire of entertainment; she could afford a life of ease, luxury, and games. But she became a follower of Jesus, sold everything to support the poor, and started the first hospital. Fabiola is regarded as the first female physician in Italy; she's almost like the early church's version of Mother Teresa.

Jerome, one of our church fathers, wrote about her. He said,

> Often did she carry on her own shoulders persons infected with jaundice or with filth. Often too did she wash away the matter discharged from wounds which others, even though men, could not bear to look at. She gave food to her patients with her own hand, and moistened the scarce breathing lips of the dying with sips of liquid.[6]

Monks in the monastic movement learned from her and went on to establish hospitals in various cities around the world.

session four **learn**

LIVING LIKE YOU CANNOT LOSE

READ ACTS 5:17-42.

How would you live if you knew you could not lose? What things would you dare and risk? What would you reach for? Whom would you reach for? What would you be brave enough to let go of for something better? What conversations would you finally have that you have been too afraid to enter into? What changes would you make in your life?

Take a few minutes to consider the questions above. How would you live if you knew you couldn't lose? Write any answers that come to mind below.

The early church lived like she could not lose.

You could not threaten her enough to quiet her.

You could not persecute her enough to still her.

You could not take enough from her to make her stop being generous.

She was kingdom-centric in a world of empire. The book of Acts provides story after story, snapshot after snapshot, of a people who fiercely loved the living God and served as His witnesses (*martyres*) in word and deed. We see one of these snapshots in Acts 5:17-42, the passage you just read.⁷

The early followers of Jesus would not stop telling the good news of the resurrected Jesus in Jerusalem. The same SANHEDRIN that presided over Jesus's arrest, trial, and crucifixion had His early followers arrested and jailed. They told the early church to stop proclaiming Jesus's name among the people. But the early church refused to be silent, and the Sanhedrin wanted to kill them.

Jesus's followers bore witness in life.

And they were unafraid to bear witness in death.

> THE ANVIL OUTLIVES THE HAMMER.⁹
>
> *A Hidden Life,* movie

But Gamaliel the Elder, a very wise and influential man in the first-century Jewish world, spoke up. It is difficult for us to understand just how important he was in his own day in Jerusalem. He was a Pharisee and a very learned rabbi. He was the first scholar of Jewish law who was ever called "Rabban," meaning "master teacher," a title greater than rabbi.⁸ The apostle Paul learned at Gamaliel's feet (Acts 22:3). To top it all off, Gamaliel was the grandson of Hillel, one of the most famous rabbis of Israel to this very day.

It seems Gamaliel saw clearly the powerful fusion of the teachings of Jesus with the flame of the Holy Spirit in these Jesus-followers. He addressed the Sanhedrin with these words:

> Therefore, in the present case I advise you: Leave these men alone! Let them go! For if their purpose or activity is of human origin, it will fail. But if it is from God, you will not be able to stop these men; you will only find yourselves fighting against God.
> ACTS 5:38-39

These wise words sum up the grit and glory of the early church from Jerusalem, Judea, Samaria, and unto the ends of the earth. These believers just kept going.

The apostle Paul captured this posture, attitude, and disposition of living like you couldn't lose in Philippians 1:20-21. He said,

> I eagerly expect and hope that I will in no way be ashamed, but will have sufficient courage so that now as always Christ will be exalted in my body, whether by life or by death. For to me, to live is Christ and to die is gain.

In other words, Paul basically said, *Let me live, and I'll keep preaching. Kill me, and I'll be with Jesus.* Either way, he couldn't lose. What do you do with people who live like this? They won't be quiet, and they won't sit down. The gospel was moving on the ground through them, and the watching world knew it.

You are invited to find out for yourself. You are invited to live with the grit and glory of the kingdom of God inside you. Your words matter. Your deeds matter. Your words and deeds unified by the teachings of Jesus and the flame of the Holy Spirit can change the world around you.

We stand on the shoulders of Telemachus, Polycarp, Fabiola, and so many others. They were witnesses in their generations. It's our turn.

How can the grit and glory of the kingdom of God show up in your life this week?

What is one thing you can do this week to live like you can't lose?

What is the one thing you need to let go of today to live like you can't lose?

Name one person you can reach out to this week to bear witness to God's work in your life.

session four **live**

*Ruins of the Palestra (a wrestling school or gymnasium) in Peloponnese, Greece

A GREAT CLOUD OF WITNESSES

Therefore, since we are surrounded by such a great cloud of witnesses [*martyres*], let us throw off everything that hinders and the sin that so easily entangles. And let us run with perseverance the race marked out for us, fixing our eyes on Jesus, the pioneer and perfecter of faith. For the joy set before him he endured the cross, scorning its shame, and sat down at the right hand of the throne of God. Consider him who endured such opposition from sinners, so that you will not grow weary and lose heart.
HEBREWS 12:1-3

In light of what we have already learned in this biblical journey together, what sticks out to you in this passage?

Hebrews 12 begins with the word *therefore*. When you see the word *therefore* in the Bible, you have to pause and read what came right before it because *therefore* is a connector. In this instance, *therefore* connects Hebrews 11 to Hebrews 12:1-3.

READ HEBREWS 11. (IT'S A PRETTY EPIC CHAPTER OF THE BIBLE; YOU MIGHT EVEN WANT TO READ IT OUT LOUD.)

Hebrews 11 is sometimes called the great "Hall of Faith" chapter. The greats throughout Israel's history are listed along with how they faith-ed. Biblical faith is not just about what you believe; it's about what you do. It's not so much a matter of having faith. It's about "verb-ing" your faith—living out the way of Jesus right in the middle of the way of the world.

In the Western world, we prioritize the following in our faith practice:

- Belief (mental assent);
- Doctrine;
- Orthodoxy (right thinking).

But in the Middle Eastern world, they prioritize these elements in their faith practice:

- Action (embodiment);
- Walking the path of *shalom;*
- Orthopraxy (right living).

This Hebrews 12 passage is all about the exercise of your faith. To me, this passage is one of the most interesting passages in the entire New Testament! Why? Because the author of Hebrews, a kingdom person, used the empire illustrations of stadium, arena, and amphitheater to teach a beautiful, hopeful kingdom of God truth.

OLYMPIC IMAGERY IN THE BIBLE

Any early New Testament reader of Hebrews 12 would have immediately thought of the Olympiad and the famous races of the Greeks. The Olympic Games started some 2,700 years ago in Olympia, an ancient city in southwest Greece. The first games were around 776 BC and ended there in Olympia around AD 393. For over a thousand years, people from around the Greek world gathered at Olympia for the games.

The games were of such importance that all Greek city-states declared a truce for one to three months around the time of the games. When everyone gathered for the

✴ (top) Vaulted entrance to the stadium at Olympia
✴ (left) Amphora vessel given as a prize, showing a foot race
✴ (right) Starting line at the ancient stadium at Olympia

Kingdom of Abundance & Empire of Scarcity 105

great competition, peace was ensured so that all could enjoy, whether they were spectating in the stands or participating in the games.

The games were held every four years. For the first twelve years of the Olympic Games, running was the only sport. Later, other sports were added. The ancient Games were part of a religious festival in honor of Zeus, king of the gods in the Greek pantheon. They believed he lived on Mount Olympus, and they competed for him, in honor of him.

The original Olympic Games allowed only free Greek males to compete, and they did so in the nude. The word *gymnasium* comes from the Greek word *gymnos* which means "naked."[10] They would oil their bodies so they would glisten in the sun. The winners did not receive gold, silver, and bronze medals as they do in today's Olympic games. Instead, they competed for the beloved and highly esteemed laurel wreath made from the leaves of the sacred olive trees at Olympia where Zeus's temple was.

This Olympic race gives us context for the imagery of Hebrews 12. And yet, the author uses this illustration to describe something entirely different, a kingdom of God encouraging and spurring on the reader. We have had so many spiritual forefathers and foremothers go before us. They lived the way of Jesus right in the middle of the watching pagan world. They ran their races.

Paul also used this imagery several times throughout the New Testament. Paul ran his race.

Telemachus ran his race and died in an arena.

Polycarp ran his race and was burned at the stake.

Fabiola ran her race in the heart of Rome and founded the first hospital there.

On and on.

Now, according to the author of Hebrews, they are sitting in the stands of a great *stadion*, also known as an arena or amphitheater.[11] And they are spectating, watching us as we run our races below. They are cheering us on. They are encouraging us to keep going, to courage up, to set our faces like flint because Jesus is worth it.

Surrounded by these witnesses (*martyres*), we take heart.[12] We throw off the things that hinder us, and we run with perseverance. With the saints behind us and our eyes fixed on Jesus, we run. We live the way of Jesus in the midst of the watching world today. It's our turn to participate.

We do not run for Zeus but for the living God. We do not go to Olympia or any sacred ritual site. We run the race in our everyday, average, mundane life. We run it at our kitchen tables, around our firepits, in our neighborhoods, churches, vocations, in the carpool line, and sitting at the executive table. We do not run for a laurel wreath but for the glory of God to be made known in the earth.

The grit and glory of the church are for the glory of God. And it's our privilege to pursue it.

Does the idea that the saints of old are cheering you on as you run your race encourage you? Why or why not?

How does the "by faith" testimony of the saints mentioned in Hebrews 11 spur you on in your walk with God? Explain.

How does remembering that your everyday faithfulness gives glory to God affect the way you approach the mundane?

Kingdom of Togetherness & Empire of Separation

ORPHANS FIND SONSHIP AT THE TABLE

SESSION FIVE

Last session, we learned more in-depth what Jesus meant in Acts 1:8 when He told His followers that they would be His "witnesses" in Jerusalem, Judea, Samaria, and unto the ends of the earth. They would bear witness to the gospel of Jesus in both life and death. All would be witnesses. Some would be martyrs.

We learned about Polycarp, an eighty-six-year-old disciple of the apostle John who died at the stake because he would not recant his faith in Jesus. He was an early church martyr, but he would not be the last.

These members of the early church knew from the very beginning that following the way of Jesus and the kingdom of God would bring great difficulty, persecution, harassment, and even death in their Roman world. The kingdom of relinquishment was thrown like mustard seed into the empire of acquisition, and the world would never be the same. While Rome sought to rule, the followers of Jesus sought to serve. Men and women, wearied by entertainment and emaciated by scarcity, found *shalom*, wholeness, abundance, and delight among the followers of Jesus. This week, we will learn more about where they found this wholeness, or *shalom*, at a particular place or setting among the early Christians.

We learned about Antioch on the Orontes and some of the things the followers of Jesus were doing there to earn them the name Christian for the first time. The pagan world gave them that name. They were known as "atheists" and "heretics" because they did not participate in the imperial cult. The world worshiped the emperor. The Christians worshiped Jesus alone.

We have seen the kingdom of celebration invading the empire of entertainment. We have seen the kingdom of abundance invading the empire of scarcity. The kingdom of God is like a mustard seed. When mustard seed hits the ground, it starts spreading, moving out and moving on. We are seeing Jesus's words in Acts 1:8 coming true as we make our way through the book of Acts.

This week, we will see the kingdom of togetherness invading the empire of separation. We might be surprised to learn what the central practice and ritual of the early church actually was in the first few centuries of the church. In the highly stratified social world of the Roman Empire, the followers of Jesus came together, cutting across racial lines, ethnic barriers, religious differences, and class distinctions. The Roman world sought to put each person in his/her place. The followers of Jesus were adamant about gathering at one place often, as a way of life. Today, we will find out where they met.

This week, we will see just how powerful one life—one kingdom mustard seed—would be in the Roman world. Paul, a learned Jewish Pharisee and follower of Jesus, would bring the gospel on the ground to one of the highest government officials named in the New Testament and cause a kingdom-of-God ruckus in one of the empire's greatest cities—Ephesus.

Today this gospel-gorgeous story continues.

We'll continue looking at snapshots through the book of Acts alongside early church histories. This living, breathing story continues in you and me. We are the current witnesses. The gospel is moving along the ground through you and me.

Peter, Paul, James, Telemachus, Polycarp, Fabiola, and many others took the kingdom adventure that came to them. Their stories are still being told. As we take the kingdom adventures that come to us, we live with deep meaning in a world of meaninglessness. And we, too, are gathering our kingdom stories.

As we begin our biblical feast, before you watch the video teaching, take a few moments to answer the following questions.

When you hear the phrase "kingdom of togetherness," what comes to your mind?

When you hear the phrase "empire of separation," what comes to your mind?

If you had to guess, what do you think was the central practice of the earliest followers of Jesus during the first few centuries of the church? Why?

Have you seen the Lord bring restoration, renewal, and repair to anything or anyone this past week? What happened?

Kingdom of Togetherness & Empire of Separation

Watch

SESSION FIVE

#GospelOnTheGround

THE FEAST

Use the following notes and space provided during our feast-teaching time. Feel free to add your own notes as you watch.

Jesus spent the vast majority of His life within a one-hundred-mile radius of where He was born. Yet His name is spoken and known in every corner of the earth. This is the story of how it happened—and is still happening.

Roman culture was highly socially-stratified, hierarchal, and status-conscious.

Roman citizens could not be crucified. Jesus was most likely seen as a plebeian or just below. This is why He was crucified as a criminal at the conviction of Pontius Pilate.

Handwritten notes:

5 people within the Roman Empire of seperation
1. Senatorial class - by their clothing
   Broad purple sash
   ← remember Lydia. She sold these sashes
2. Equestrian
   - thinner purple sash
3. Aristocratic
   - white collar
   - wealthier
4. Plebian
   - blue collar
   - free
5. Slave

* How was the church different
* Status mattered, someone on top, stuck with your own group
* 1/3 of the empire were slaves

Crusifiction is humiliating

* If you want to see Jesus - Go LOW
* Look at new testament scripture in this Roman culture
* Jesus would have been in the lower class

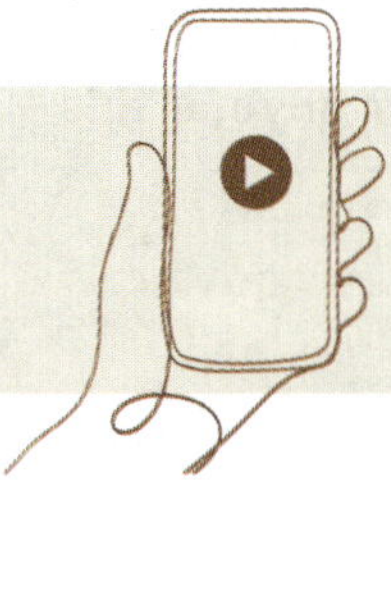

TO ACCESS THE VIDEO TEACHING SESSIONS,
USE THE INSTRUCTIONS IN THE BACK OF YOUR BIBLE STUDY BOOK.

The church starts mixing the order

The DIDACHE was discovered in 1873 by Philotheos Bryennios.
— Look up ↓ came from a poor family

↳ means teachings
↳ the manual of the early church. How to live as a follower of Jesus ← These have been found
Be generous - look at this guy
Talked about what they were to do when eating at the table

Jesus spent a lot of time engaging people through table fellowship. The early church followed Jesus's model of vibrant, regular table fellowship.
how shallow

★ table fellowship was important
  James 2 - do not show favoritism
★ Table of God, we sit shoulder to shoulder
      WE ARE UNIFIED
    Food - fellowship ♡
          Love

Table fellowship is subversive to the way of empire / the individualistic, hurried way of the world.

☀ Matthew 11:18 - He loves to eat with the lowly
  Acts 2:42-47 Companion - derives from together + bread
  People sell their houses to help one another
       Who eats at my table?
      my brothers + sisters   Isaiah 25:6-8

Every time we eat together, we are practicing for the wedding supper of the Lamb. ★ DIVERSITY   It's not just about family

★ Don't invite family + friends to the table
Sin entered the world through eating
  ↳ THEN marriage supper
     1 Corinthians 11:17-34 ♥

Kingdom of Togetherness & Empire of Separation   113

session five **discuss**

LET'S YESHIVA!

Take some time to discuss the following questions with your group:

What is the most surprising thing that you learned this week in our video teaching?

Do you feel like your life is currently more anchored in the empire of separation or the kingdom of togetherness? Why?

A wealthy family funded a scholarship so Philotheos Bryennios could go to seminary. He would go on to discover the Didache!

Who has been generous toward you along the way in your life? Take a few moments to tell your group about him/her and what a difference he/she made. (You might also want to reach out to him/her this week to share what his/her kindness meant to you.)

Whom can you be generous toward this week? Brainstorm some ideas in your group, and then on your own. Pick one to carry out. Take that step of generosity this week. Reach out and meet a tangible need in someone's life.

What are your current table fellowship practices?

How can you be more intentional to use your dining table as an instrument for the kingdom of God?

THE GOSPEL ON THE GROUND

Prayer requests

Michelle - Praise he is done with job
Appyling for jobs / got called for one
Caroline - Praise for dogs
getting drivers license
Sonni - Safe travels for the weekend
everything coming together
for clarity & provisions in these situations.

session five **follow-up**

THE SEAT OF HONOR

READ 1 CORINTHIANS 11:17-24 AND JAMES 2:1-4.

Compare the two passages in the chart below.

Differences between the two passages	Similarities between the two passages

As you likely noted in your chart above, both of these passages have to do with seats of honor, social status, and table fellowship.

In light of what we learned at this week's feast, what sticks out to you in this passage?

The books of 1 Corinthians and James were penned by two different human authors, Paul and James, respectively, under the inspiration of the Holy Spirit. It seems like God really wanted to make sure to get this message across, seeing as it was repeated twice and emphasized by two very different authors.

Why do you think addressing this issue was so important to the early church? Feel free to guess if you're not sure you know the exact answer.

✻ The Library of Celsus was the third-largest library in the Roman world.

Kingdom of Togetherness & Empire of Separation

The early church's practice of meeting together was not without its risks and cost. In fact, the kingdom of togetherness so flew in the face of the empire of separation that it became a point of persecution.

History and historical documents are gifts to us from God because they can give us insight into the cultural undertones of the first century. To help us understand a bit of the struggle that early church members went through, read this excerpt from a historic letter between **PLINY THE YOUNGER**, governor of Pontus and Bithynia from AD 111–113, and Trajan, the emperor of Rome from AD 98–117.

The government of Rome, the emperor himself, struggled to know how to handle the gospel of Jesus Christ spreading through its empire. These early followers refused to stop meeting together and refused to worship at the imperial cult—and many paid the ultimate price.

But God was their reward and His dwelling place their home. This gospel mustard seed was moving along the ground, and it was not about to stop growing.

✶ The triclinium featured a couch extending around three sides of a table used by the ancient Romans for reclining at meals.

> **Companion**
>
> *com* – with
> *panis* – bread
>
> Your companion is whom you break bread with[1].

118   THE GOSPEL ON THE GROUND

PLINY TO THE EMPEROR TRAJAN

Meanwhile, in the case of those who were denounced to me as Christians, I have observed the following procedure: I interrogated these as to whether they were Christians; those who confessed I interrogated a second and third time, threatening them with punishment; those who persisted I ordered executed. For I had no doubt that, whatever the nature of their creed, stubbornness and inflexible obstinacy surely deserve to be punished.

. . . An anonymous document was published containing the names of many persons. Those who denied that they were or had been Christians, when they invoked the gods in words dictated by me, offered prayer with incense and wine to your image, which I had ordered to be brought for this purpose together with statues of the gods, and moreover cursed Christ—none of which those who are really Christians, it is said, can be forced to do—these I thought should be discharged.

. . . They asserted, however, that the sum and substance of their fault or error had been that they were accustomed to meet on a fixed day before dawn and sing responsively a hymn to Christ as to a god, and to bind themselves by oath. . . . Accordingly, I judged it all the more necessary to find out what the truth was by torturing two female slaves who were called deaconesses. But I discovered nothing else but depraved, excessive superstition.

TRAJAN TO PLINY

. . . if they are denounced [to you as Christians] and proved guilty, they are to be punished, with this reservation, that whoever denies that he is a Christian and really proves it—that is, by worshiping our gods—even though he was under suspicion in the past, shall obtain pardon through repentance.[2]

(Pliny *Letters* 10.96–7)

session five **look**

※ Ruins of Corinth with acropolis on to of the mountain in the background

PAUL IN THE CITIES OF APHRODITE AND ARTEMIS

READ ACTS 18:1-4.

What do we learn about Paul in these verses?

Whom is he partnering with and what does he have in common with them?

It is difficult to truly grasp the gospel impact that the apostle Paul made throughout the Roman Empire in the first-century AD. The depth of discipleship and the breadth of geography he traveled is really mind-blowing. Paul is one of the greatest examples in church history of someone who embodied the idea that the kingdom of God is like a mustard seed.

Life with Paul would have felt like many things I'm sure, but *boring* is not a word we would use. Every day with Paul would have been an adventure, whether sailing on a ship, walking a Roman road, teaching in synagogues, or debating scholars on Mars Hill in Athens. At the same time, one of his most fruitful daily ministry posts would have been the leather shop where he would have worked in Corinth and Ephesus.

Paul was a Jewish Pharisee and a Roman citizen. He would have been a member of the PLEBEIAN class (lower class) within the Empire. We often think of

Paul as a revered scholar and powerful disciple of Jesus. And in the Jewish world, he was considered highly-educated and well-respected. When he entered the Jewish synagogues to teach, he was revered. But in the economic and social status of the Roman world, he was in low standing. He would have likely been considered inconsequential to the Roman elite.

Acts 18 tells us that Paul was a "tentmaker." The Greek word for *tentmaker* is *skēnopoios,* which refers to a leatherworker.³ Remember from our earlier discussion, Joseph and Jesus were carpenters—*tektōns*—stonemasons.⁴

Paul was a leatherworker in the Empire; he was lowly within the world of Rome. But the living God always has a way of taking the least and making the most out of them. No one in the first-century world would have ever thought that a Jewish Rabbi could be the Savior of the world. And no one would have ever guessed that a plebeian tentmaker would shake the empire to its very core.

As a leatherworker, Paul would have traveled with his tools everywhere he went. When he arrived in a new city, he would often visit the local synagogue first. His next stop would be the *agora* (or marketplace) to meet with the other leatherworkers in that city. In antiquity, you could not survive on your own. People within a certain vocation would seek to join a *collegia* (college) or guild. Guilds functioned like ancient vocational fraternities or unions.⁵ People would band together, work together, and help take care of one another as a safety net against things like misfortune, illness, or financial difficulties.

That's exactly what we see Paul doing in Acts 18. Upon his arrival in Corinth, we imagine he went to the local *agora* and met two other leatherworkers—Priscilla and Aquila. They worked together, most likely within a *collegia* or guild. Paul not only shared his vocational trade with Priscilla and Aquila, but he also shared his faith in Jesus.

As leatherworkers, in addition to tents, they would have made things like leather boots, wineskins, awnings, and

In the first-century world, Sadducees were the wealthy, religious elite. They collaborated with the Roman Empire and were not thought of favorably by the Jewish people. Pharisees, on the other hand, were well-educated in the ways of God but usually of a lower economic status. They all had jobs to support themselves and their families—jobs like farmer, smelter, carpenter, or herdsman.

Kingdom of Togetherness & Empire of Separation

gladiatorial outfits. Leatherworkers were despised and frowned upon in the ancient world because they used urine to soak and stretch the leather. It was considered a dirty, unclean vocation.

The largest cities throughout the Roman Empire had patron deities or gods. The patron god or goddess was thought to provide protection, provision, and notoriety for that city. The people within that city would worship the emperor (we've already talked about the imperial cult) and the patron god or goddess of the city. The patron goddess of Corinth in the first-century world of Paul was Aphrodite. A temple was built in her honor on top of the acropolis at Corinth. Those ruins are still there to this day along with the ruins of the *agora* (marketplace).

We can imagine what worship of Aphrodite would have been like when visiting her temple. Corinth, a major city in the Roman Empire in the first century, had it all—slave trade, brothels, rowdy sailors who had come to port, goods traded from all over the empire, wealth, and open sexuality, just to name a few. The city of Corinth even hosted the Isthmian games, a Roman version of the Greek Olympic games.

Paul spent eighteen months in this city and this culture, contending for the way of Jesus within the way of Aphrodite (Acts 18:11). If you thought Paul, Priscilla, and Aquila made a kingdom impact in Corinth, just wait for what happened later with Paul in Ephesus!

READ ACTS 19.

For me, the events of Acts 19 provide an excellent snapshot of the book of Acts as a whole. The gospel is not stagnant. It moves. It's alive. It travels. There is nowhere it is afraid to enter into and settle within to bring salvation and restoration.

Let's unpack a few of the big moments together.

Focusing on verses 11-20, list below the big elements of this story.

> THE GOSPEL IS NOT STAGNANT. IT MOVES. IT'S ALIVE. IT TRAVELS. THERE IS NOWHERE IT IS AFRAID TO ENTER INTO AND SETTLE WITHIN TO BRING SALVATION AND RESTORATION.

In verse 20, what does the Bible attribute these miracles to?

Paul arrived in Ephesus. He went to the synagogue first and started visiting the lecture hall of Tyrannus daily (vv. 8-10). He did this for two years! He was a leatherworker by day and was leading a Bible study at night. The Lord started working miracles through Paul, so much so that sorcerers in the city even brought their scrolls and burned them in open confession and repentance. They not only burned them; they burned them publicly (vv. 17-20).

Scrolls were expensive in the ancient world, and it was often a sign of some measure of wealth to own scrolls. The sum total value of the scrolls burned was fifty thousand *drachmas*—the equivalent to fifty thousand days' wages![6] This was an incredibly open and expensive confession.

The four largest and most influential cities in the Roman Empire during the first century were Rome, Alexandria, Antioch on the Orontes, and Ephesus. In a world without electricity, ancient street lamps—torches positioned along

Kingdom of Togetherness & Empire of Separation

their major streets—gave light in the night to these beautiful, wealthy imperial cities.

When I take teams to Turkey and Greece, we visit ancient Ephesus. She is beautiful to this very day. Her major streets are made of marble. You can still sit in the enormous theater that held twenty-five-thousand people in the first century. This theater is the theater of the riot in Acts 19.

Ephesus was home to one of the seven wonders of the ancient world—the Greek temple of Artemis known as the Artemisium. At Ephesus, it was all about Artemis. She was considered the mother goddess and is often portrayed as multi-breasted, a symbol meant to indicate she fed the world. The Romans called her Diana.

The Artemisium was one of the most glorious man-made achievements in human history at that time, boasting 127 columns. Today, one single column remains. It is striking to stand there with a team, seeing the ruins of one of the seven wonders of the ancient world. It is such a visual reminder of how the empires of the world will fade over time, but the kingdom of God lives forever and ever. No ruins or the sad remnant remains of past glory will be in heaven.

People traveled from around the world to Ephesus to worship Artemis. The citizens of Ephesus were directly, immediately, and faithfully connected to their patron goddess Artemis. They were emotionally connected to her as well. They loved her. They were loyal to her. She wasn't just Artemis. She was Artemis of the Ephesians.

Because people came from near and far to visit the Artemisium, the economy of Ephesus was centered on the worship of Artemis. When your worship and your economy are tied to Artemis, you will protect her at any cost. Silversmiths and artisans of all kinds created and sold statues of Artemis and little figurines among other things. Whole vocations and guilds in Ephesus were built around Artemis and solely funded by goods made in her image and in her honor.

With that historical context in mind, let's jump back to Acts 19, this time focusing on verses 23-41.

In verse 24, whom do we meet and what are we told about his occupation?

What was this person upset about, and how did he try to address his concern?

What do you think his motive was?

Acts 19 continues with a man named Demetrius, a silversmith and a member of the silversmith collegia, or guild, in Ephesus. They were the ones who made the Artemis figurines and statues to sell to the city and the world as they visited the Artemisium.

Demetrius saw the writing on the wall. As the gospel grew in Ephesus, the Artemis profits started dwindling. The gospel was putting Artemis out of business in her own city! So he brought together the other silversmiths and artisans in their guild (vv. 25-27) and said if Paul was allowed to continue teaching in the city, their guild would go bankrupt and Artemis herself would lose her great name. This caused an uproar throughout the entire city as people flocked to the twenty-five thousand seat theater. For two hours they shouted in unison, "Great is Artemis of the Ephesians!" (v. 28).

Can you feel the tension, the fear, and the madness of the mob? Ephesus was turned upside down, and Paul, our kingdom mustard seed in Ephesus, wanted to go into the theater and address the crowd (vv. 30-31). Thankfully Paul's disciples prevented him from going in, and we're told the town clerk helped calm the crowd and dismiss the assembly (vv. 35-41).

At this point in the story, one thing was clear. No city in the entire Roman Empire would be immune to the power of the gospel and the followers of Jesus living within her walls.

I imagine Ephesus on an ordinary night some two thousand years ago. I imagine her marbled streets glowing by the firelight of the torches along the way. I imagine how strong and secure, wealthy and proud she must have felt with the mighty Artemis thought to be watching over the city. And I imagine Paul, a Jewish leatherworker, a plebeian, walking into the great city for the first time, holding his bag of tools and a water wineskin with a slight smile on his face. No one probably would have ever given Paul a second look or a second thought. He would have arrived as a total nobody to the Ephesians; they all would have looked right past him.

But in time, they all would know his name. And more importantly, they would know the name of the one true God.

session five **learn**

* Ruins of a theater at Corinth

A PLEBEIAN AND A PROCONSUL AT THE TABLE OF WELCOME

READ ACTS 13:4-12.

The Bible was given to us so that we might know who the living God is, what He is like, and what it looks like to walk with Him. One of the things we learn about the Lord in the book of Acts is that He is coming for everyone! His table of welcome is huge, and He's inviting the world to come to His table through His people, His ambassadors.

> We are therefore Christ's ambassadors, as though God were making his appeal through us.
> **2 CORINTHIANS 5:20a**

As we have seen, no city in the Roman Empire was immune to the power of the gospel and the kingdom of God within her walls. No one would have ever dreamed that the mighty Aphrodite and Artemis would be so effectively upended by a ragtag group of lower class, plebeian, simple men and women who followed and worshiped Jesus of Nazareth. The might of empire was being shaken by the presence of the kingdom of God, upended by the followers of Jesus and their daily fidelity to the way of Jesus in the world of Caesar and Rome. The gospel was moving along the ground.

Kingdom of Togetherness & Empire of Separation

Thinking back to the Acts 13 passage that you just read, answer the following questions:

Who summoned Barnabas and Saul after "they had gone through the whole island as far as Paphos" (v. 6, ESV), and what did he want?

Describe the confrontation that happened between Elymas/Bar-Jesus and Saul. In the end, what was the result?

The book of Acts reads like an action movie. So many incredible gospel stories, one right after another. The kingdom was on the move!

You may have noticed we consistently see the presence of magic and sorcerers in the book of Acts.

- Simon the Sorcerer in Samaria—Acts 8
- Bar-Jesus the Sorcerer in Paphos—Acts 13
- People practicing sorcery in Ephesus—Acts 19

Again and again, the followers of Jesus not only interacted with the people of empire, but they also contended against the kingdom of darkness itself. Dark and light were colliding. The kingdom of darkness was being invaded by the kingdom of light. Followers of Jesus were inviting the world to come into the light and to take their seats at the table of welcome.

In Acts 13, the power of Elymas/Bar-Jesus the sorcerer ran into the power of God in Paul and, as you read, Elymas ended up blind, groping around because he was "not even able to see the light of the sun" (13:11).

And then, we read,

> When the proconsul saw what had happened, he believed, for he was amazed at the teaching about the Lord.
> ACTS 13:12

Watching this showdown between magic and kingdom led to the first-named convert of Paul in the New Testament. And what a convert he was! His name was SERGIUS PAULUS, and he was a proconsul in the Roman Empire.

It is hard for us to understand exactly how powerful and influential a proconsul was within the government of Rome. A proconsul would be the modern-day equivalent of a cabinet member who advises the president or a cardinal who gives wise counsel to the pope. For a bit of a larger context, you may remember that the Gospels tell us Pontius Pilate was a prefect of Judea (Luke 3:1). A prefect would have operated like a ruler of a county in a state. In contrast, a proconsul would be like the governor of an entire state (multiple counties). Much in the same way that governors today interact with the president, a proconsul would have interacted with the emperor of the Roman Empire.

Sergius Paulus was the highest-ranking government official named as a follower of Jesus in the entire New Testament. Now we understand why Luke found it so important to provide his name as he was writing the book of Acts. Paul had many converts, but this one was unusual.

You may notice that Saul's name was changed to Paul—the Bible specifically mentions it in Acts 13:9. Most usually understand this mention as a change associated with Paul's conversion, and it's just as likely that Saul was his Hebrew name and Paul was his Greek/Roman name. However, I find it interesting to note the connection between Paulus and Paul. Perhaps Paul was somewhat affiliating his name with the powerful Sergius Paulus in the same way he affiliated with the powerful Gamaliel the Elder back in Jerusalem.

The gospel was moving powerfully throughout the geography of the empire and up its imperial chain of command. By Acts 13, we have a proconsul follower of Jesus who interacted with the emperor of Rome. The gospel was getting closer and closer to the very heart of the empire—the city of Rome and the Caesar living within her walls.

Who is the living God? He's the One who is coming for everyone!

No one expected a plebeian, urine-stained Jewish leatherworker to lead a proconsul of the Roman Empire to the Lord and invite him to take his seat at the table of welcome. But such is the kingdom of God.

session five **live**

* Roman communal kitchen. Grates were placed on top over burning coals.

The table of welcome was open to the world as the followers of Jesus lived and proclaimed the *ratzon l'adonai* to everyone they met.[7,8] Their lives were marked by invitation. They interacted with the Roman world, not with harsh judgment but with a warm welcome.

They had taken their seats at the table of welcome and knew the *shalom*, harmony, and wholeness that comes from walking with Jesus. They wanted others to know it too.

SPIRITUAL HYGIENE

This week we have read and studied several stories through the book of Acts. The kingdom of togetherness was invading the empire of separation. Roman imperial cities like Corinth and Ephesus were being deeply impacted and transformed by the gospel message of Jesus and the power of the Holy Spirit living inside the followers of Jesus within their walls. High-ranking officials in the government of the Roman Empire were becoming followers of Jesus.

The kingdom was truly advancing like a mustard seed, just as Jesus said. The gospel was moving on the ground from Jerusalem to Judea, Samaria, and unto the ends of the earth, just as Jesus said. Acts 1:8 was coming true chapter by chapter, verse by verse, story by story, one city at a time, and one life at a time.

We read these miraculous, amazing, extraordinary stories, and we ask ourselves, *How shall **we** now live in light of **this**?* I read these stories in the book of Acts and then I look at my own life, and it seems like they could not be more different. Paul was challenging the Artemis cult in Ephesus, and I spent today weeding my backyard, paying a few bills, returning phone calls, and answering emails. Nothing spectacular is going on here in my world. I'm pretty sure nothing about me is going to cause a gospel riot in my city today.

The book of Acts reads so extraordinarily. My life feels so ordinary. Acts reads like a movie in fast-forward. My life feels relatively slow-paced most days. So how do I apply the book of Acts to my life when it seems I don't have much in common with Paul, Priscilla, and Aquila?

When we look closer, we find that we do share something significant with them. Our lives as followers of Jesus are similar to the lives they lived two thousand years ago in some very small yet powerful ways. Because of those similarities, we can see ourselves in them and live with hopeful expectancy that the living God is partnering with *us* in our own day and generation to bring restoration, renewal, and repair in the world. We are living out this continued story of the gospel moving on the ground, and we are collecting our own snapshots and stories of God's presence, power, and ministry to the world through us.

What is the commonality between them and us?

They practiced daily spiritual hygiene.

And so do we.

Just as we take care of our bodies every day, we take care of our souls every day too. I learned the phrase "spiritual hygiene" while I was in seminary. One of my favorite textbooks was written by a man named Cornelius Plantinga, Jr. He wrote about spiritual hygiene and the small daily practices that lead to a robust, centered, and well-watered walk with Jesus.[9]

These are the small rhythms and practices that put us in God's way and put us in others' company in meaningful ways. Some of these practices are universal to followers of Jesus everywhere—Bible study, prayer, serving, and giving, for example.

But some are particular to each person. Some practices are things we do as individual expressions of *shalom*, wholeness, and delight with the living God and with others.

Three practices have become vital in my walk with Jesus. They are consistent and quiet. The presence of the living God in these things centers me, guides me, and funds my life to live as a gospel witness and a kingdom mustard seed in the earth. I'm going to share my practices with you, in the hopes that they'll be an encouragement to spur you on in your own spiritual hygiene practices.

5:00 A.M. WALKS WITH CHESTER

I get up at 5:00 a.m. every morning and go on a walk with coffee and my dog, Chester. It is a silent walk—no music, no podcasts, no sermons, no nothing.

It's just me, giving the firstfruits of my day to the living God. It is me walking with Him. I pray. I listen. I breathe. Somehow, when I return home, I know what I need to know regarding things in my life—decisions to be made, people to check on, things to do, and things to stop doing. My early morning walks with the Lord govern my life. I begin my day with Him. It is the genesis of my day, every day.

JOURNALING

Memory and stories are both sacred. They matter. They matter more than we know. Memory is a gift that allows us to keep record of God's faithfulness in our lives over time, over a lifetime. Journaling is my way of practicing sacred memory. I write, scribe, and record the stories of God's faithfulness in my life. Every December, I take three days to read through the journal I've kept for that whole year. It allows me to get up above my life and view it from thirty-five thousand feet, almost like the view from the window of an airplane. It gives me perspective and vision as I prepare to head into the new year, the next year, and the next things.

TABLE FELLOWSHIP

The early church practiced coming to the table of welcome together just as Jesus had done so often during His earthly ministry. Eating together was the common, core practice for the early church. I believe strongly in table fellowship. I actually do believe that every time we eat together, we are practicing for the wedding supper of the Lamb. I am intentional to "break bread" with people in my life. It is my opportunity to inherit the saints living around me, to be curious about them, learn their stories, share my own stories, and experience the gift of friendship and community. It is one of my most intentional hygienic practices to care for my soul.

WHAT ABOUT YOU?

What are some of your spiritual hygiene practices? This week, make a list, share them with others, and ask people in your life to share their practices with you.

Are there any spiritual hygiene practices you need to *add* to your life right now? Why?

Are there any practices that have become stale to you, practices you need to *let go* of right now? Explain.

Kingdom of Togetherness & Empire of Separation

BROTHERS AND SISTERS BOUND TOGETHER IN PRAYER AND FASTING

SESSION SIX

Last week, we learned that one of the central practices and rhythms of the early church was table fellowship. In the ancient world, who you ate with said everything about you; it was one of the highest affiliations. Eating with people signified in the culture of the day that you welcomed, embraced, and accepted them. The Roman Empire was highly stratified socially; the early church was highly unified. As the followers of Jesus were thrown like mustard seed throughout the empire, they found brotherhood, comfort, and a sense of kingdom family at the table.

In an empire of separation, they modeled the kingdom of togetherness. They powerfully saw themselves within God's family and related to one another as brothers and sisters. The table—sharing food—was one of the chief ways they gathered together, cutting across ethnic, racial, religious, class, and economic distinctions. At the table, they practiced unity in diversity, and it baffled the Roman world.

We also learned about the Didache, the practical manual of the early church. The book of Acts gives incredible insight into the daily lives of the early church, and the Didache does as well. The Didache gives practical guidelines and instructions for how to live as followers of Jesus in everyday life. It is fascinating to learn that the second largest section of the Didache deals with table fellowship.

Table fellowship is still powerful in our world today. Sin entered the world through eating. It makes sense that restoration and renewal also happen at a table. Table fellowship is subversive kingdom activity in our modern world of empire. Slowing down, setting our tables, and inviting people to them is one of the holiest things we can do—to welcome, embrace, and accept one another—to share food and stories, giving ourselves and receiving others as brothers and sisters in the Lord.

This week we will go further into the kingdom of togetherness in the midst of an empire of separation. We will learn how one became a follower of Jesus and a member of the Christian community within the Roman world. We'll also unpack how the early church welcomed and incorporated people who were interested in knowing more about the way of Jesus and the kingdom of God.

We will explore some of the other key practices and rhythms that tethered the early church to the Lord and to one another in faithful Christian community. Today we will learn about two more practices that were core, rhythmic, and calendrical for the early church. In other words, they were scheduled, marked on their calendars, and practiced regularly.

Today this gospel-gorgeous story continues. We'll continue looking at snapshots through the book of Acts alongside early church histories. We will be encouraged and challenged by the faithful witness and committed practices of the early church. The Bible was not only given to comfort us but to quicken us unto all righteousness. Let's be encouraged and challenged together, shoulder-to-shoulder as sisters in God's family.

We are not only going to learn about some of these early church practices and rhythms, but we are also going to actually have an opportunity to practice them together this week! We are going to embody these things, not just carry them around in our heads. We are going to get a small taste of what kingdom life would have been like for them.

As we begin our biblical feast, before you watch the video teaching, take a few moments to answer the following questions.

We learned about the importance of table fellowship last week. How would you describe table fellowship in your life right now?

Is it a normal practice? How do you practice it? Who tends to eat with you?

Have you ever experienced unusual restoration through eating with others?

How have you lived like a mustard seed, spreading the kingdom of God, this past week?

Have you seen the Lord bring restoration, renewal, and repair to anything or anyone this past week?

Watch

SESSION SIX

#GospelOnTheGround

Two rhythms of Jesus followers

THE FEAST

Use the following notes and space provided during our feast-teaching time. Feel free to add your own notes as you watch.

Jesus spent the vast majority of His life within a one-hundred-mile radius of where He was born. Yet His name is spoken and known in every corner of the earth. This is the story of how it happened—and is still happening.

Live like you cannot lose

When one became a follower of Jesus, he/she was joined to Jesus and a community. Individual salvation brought someone into the communal faith.

Communal faith comes first?
Jesus came to have a group that could go to the Father
★ Need to have communal faith
Me → We

Jesus addressed three practices in the Sermon on the Mount: giving, prayer, and fasting.

THIS ☆ Jesus did not save me so that I could come up with what I believe and who gets saved
1. Giving
2. Prayer } important
3. Fasting

TO ACCESS THE VIDEO TEACHING SESSIONS,
USE THE INSTRUCTIONS IN THE BACK OF YOUR BIBLE STUDY BOOK.

handwritten: I corinthian 3:16 - I am a ~~tab~~ temple - The you's are plural

Giving, praying, and fasting were regular practices. They were also communal practices, not just individualistic practices.

handwritten: prayer - [OUR] father, [YOUR] name
I Peter 2:4-5 - A living stone in the spiritual house to be a HOLY priesthood

handwritten: We need all the living stones

The Jewish people regularly prayed at 9:00 a.m. and 3:00 p.m.
The Jewish people regularly fasted on Mondays and Thursdays.

handwritten:
* For encouraging each other
* Did this when they couldn't share space, they started to share time
* The same prayer - Shohma
No hebrew for the word obey - to hear is to do ↑ Shohma in hebrew
Love your neighbor as yourself

The early church regularly prayed at 9:00 a.m., 12:00 p.m., and 3:00 p.m. The followers of Jesus regularly fasted on Wednesdays and Fridays. *handwritten:* Reminder

handwritten: Why do I not do this?

These rhythms and practices of fasting held them together in profoundly powerful ways. How would it impact your week to pratice these things?

session six **discuss**

LET'S YESHIVA!

Take some time to discuss the following questions with your group:

What did you just hear or see in our feast together that you want to remember?

This will give us a powerful way to "get into the shoes" of our brothers and sisters in the early church and experience the communal faith similar to the ways they experienced it two thousand years ago.

Daily Prayer:
9:00 a.m., 12:00 p.m., 3:00 p.m.

The Lord's Prayer

What do you think about how people interested in the way of Jesus would walk with a community of believers before joining the community through baptism?

Weekly Fasting*:
Wednesday and Friday

*Note: if you plan to join us in the communal rhythm of prayer and fasting this week, please go ahead and read the Live section on pages 156–158 to get started.

What do you think about how the early followers of Jesus practiced fixed times of prayer and fasting?

Will you join us in practicing fixed times of prayer and fasting this week?

Prayer requests

Michelle - Friend in Colorado expecting a baby and having health problems. May have to stay in the hospital. Another friend had a cyst on her ovaries
↳ for God's plan in Michelles life

session six **follow-up**

THE NATURAL AND SUPERNATURAL IN THE EARLY CHURCH

> **READ ACTS 20:1-12.**

When we come to Acts 20, the gospel had moved powerfully from Jerusalem, Judea, and Samaria and was well into "the ends of the earth" of the Roman Empire (Acts 1:8). The kingdom was indeed like a mustard seed just as Jesus said. Wherever the followers of Jesus went, the gospel took root and began spreading.

Acts 20 traces the movement of Paul and his companions to places throughout Macedonia and Greece.

In verse 4, we read the names and places of origin for Paul's traveling companions. In the space below, fill in the names of the cities where these men lived.

Sopater son of Pyrrhus from _____

Aristarchus and Secundus from
_____

Gaius and Timothy from _____

Tychicus and Trophimus from the _____
____ _____

> WHEREVER THE FOLLOWERS OF JESUS WENT, THE GOSPEL TOOK ROOT AND BEGAN SPREADING.

Paul's traveling buddies show us just how far the gospel had reached geographically, ethnically, and culturally.

When we come to verses 7-12, Paul and his companions were in a city called Troas. The city was another large, Hellenistic city with a population of around one hundred thousand in its heyday.[1] A port city on the Aegean Sea, many sailed to Troas

✳ Road in Troas   Kingdom of Togetherness & Empire of Separation

and stayed there before moving on to other destinations. In fact, Paul did just that on many of his travels. The ruins of the ancient bath, gymnasium, and stadium in Troas are still visible to this day.

This snapshot in Acts 20:7-12 shows us how the early church was marked by both the natural and supernatural as the gospel moved along the ground. To me, this passage is one of the funniest stories in the book of Acts—funny and powerful.

In verses 7-12, which of the rhythms that we've discussed were members of the early church practicing?

The early church cultivated the kingdom of togetherness by spending a lot of time together. As we have seen, they ate together, prayed together, fasted together, and met together often to hear from the apostles such as Paul and Peter. During these normal, natural times of togetherness, supernatural things would sometimes happen—this is exactly what we read about in this passage.

I laugh every time I tell this story and teach this passage.

The followers of Jesus in Troas were gathered together to eat (one of their central practices). Paul decided to start talking, and well, he just kept on talking. Most of us get fidgety if a sermon goes over an hour, and the passage tells us that Paul talked until midnight. How many of you would have fallen asleep, left, or just zoned out from all the talking?

Even though it was late, Paul would have likely kept on teaching except for an unusual interruption that sparked a supernatural miracle right in the middle of their meal and Bible study!

A young man was there that night whose name was Eutychus. Amazingly, the Bible gives us his name because it means "fortunate" or "lucky."[2] Eutychus was sitting in a window, and he fell asleep as Paul talked on and on. Not only did he fall asleep, but he also fell out of the third-story window and died.

Can you imagine? Can you actually try to put yourself in that room at that moment, using your Spirit-soaked imagination? How would you have responded? Maybe you would have been dozing too as Paul preached what seemed like the longest sermon ever known to man.

The followers of Jesus were doing very natural things together—eating together, listening to scriptural teaching together, and *WHAM!* There goes Eutychus. He doesn't seem so "fortunate" or "lucky" at this point in the story, does he?

THE EARLY CHURCH CULTIVATED THE KINGDOM OF TOGETHERNESS BY SPENDING A LOT OF TIME TOGETHER.

What did Paul do in this moment? Freak out? Call the first-century version of 911? No, he simply went downstairs, threw himself on Eutychus, and put his arms around him. And Eutychus was raised from the dead. Right there. Right then. A supernatural miracle visited that community right in the middle of their very natural practice of table fellowship and listening to biblical teaching. Now Eutychus's name seems a much better fit!

Can you imagine? Can you actually try to put yourself in that room at that moment in your mind's eye, and envision how you would have responded after this miracle happened? This incredible moment took place in a house in Troas, another city that so embodied empire. But the kingdom of God had taken root inside its walls, and a young man was raised from the dead.

What did Paul do next? Freak out. Call first-century 911 to get Eutychus checked out? No, he simply went back upstairs, kept eating, and kept talking until daylight. He wanted to finish his meal and finish teaching his lesson. My goodness!

It seems as if Paul wasn't phased in the least by what happened. He expected the presence of the Lord in the midst of Christian community. He knew that following Jesus was not just knowing what Jesus knew but being like Him. He knew that the kingdom of God was moving, advancing like mustard seed. Even powerful places like Troas would carry kingdom stories that happened within her walls.

Members of the early church came to eat together, hear teaching, and share in the fellowship of the saints. Instead they witnessed a dead man raised to life again. Talk about getting more than you came for. What stories they must have told their family and friends, their coworkers and neighbors. How do you think the Gentile citizens of Troas would have felt when they heard this story, met Eutychus for themselves, and listened to his testimony? Kingdom was invading empire, and death was giving way to life.

This passage ends with something so beautiful.

Fill in the missing word in the passage:

The people took the young man home alive and were greatly _____.
ACTS 20:12 (NIV)

Keep this idea of comfort in mind. We will look deeper into this concept later this week in our study.

session six **look**

PAUL AND A KINGDOM RUCKUS IN JERUSALEM

Our storyline continues from Paul and Eutychus in Troas in Acts 20 to Paul returning to Jerusalem in Acts 21. Ah, we are back to the place of origin, beginning, and genesis of the church. Jerusalem will forever be the home of Pentecost Sunday, where the Spirit fell like flame on that small band of followers of Jesus at the temple. Remember, we read about that event in Acts 2. Now we are in Acts 21 and the gospel has traveled far and wide on the ground, embodied in the lives of men and women who were living the way of kingdom in a world of empire. As the gospel moved along the ground, more and more and more Gentiles accepted Jesus as Messiah and started living as committed followers of Jesus.

Consider what it would have been like to be a Gentile living in Corinth, Athens, Rome, EPHESUS, or Troas who became a committed follower of Jesus? They would have been exchanging empire for kingdom and starting to live within a Christian community in their cities. In time, they would have probably longed to visit Jerusalem, the city where God's name dwells, to visit His temple, His house. Pilgrimage would have been sown into their hearts. They would probably have wanted to visit the land of their Messiah and to worship the living God.

They would have likely saved up money for a long time and made plans for international travel in antiquity.

Consider the sense of expectation and hopefulness as they set out.

They probably would have dreamed about what they would do when they arrived at God's house in Jerusalem.

Imagine joy and the sense of wonder that would have lived in their hearts as they moved closer and closer to Jerusalem.

We have seen the massive kingdom of God ruckus that Paul and the gospel caused in Ephesus. Artemis of the Ephesians was no match for the mustard seed of the kingdom planted within her walls by Paul, Priscilla, Aquila, and others. The whole city ended up rioting in the enormous theater at Ephesus in Acts 19.

> READ ACTS 21:17-36.

In three to four sentences, summarize the storyline and action in this passage. What exactly is happening?

Why do you think folks were so upset with Paul in verses 27-29? Take a guess based on the biblical context if you're not sure.

In Acts 21, Paul and his kingdom of togetherness practices caused a kingdom of God ruckus in Jerusalem itself. Paul had a habit of visiting the local synagogues first when he arrived in a new city or region, and he quickly started sharing the gospel hope with anyone and everyone who would listen to him. He was an ambassador to the Gentiles. Remember in Acts 20:4, we met some of Paul's travel companions, men from various cities and regions throughout the empire.

It makes perfect Pauline sense that he would bring Gentiles to Jerusalem with him, to see the incarnational space of Jesus and to worship the living God at the temple, especially considering the ways that Jesus taught His disciples—bringing them along and teaching them as they went through life together.

This is the context of our story in Acts 21.

It wasn't just the Romans who practiced social and stratified separation. Along the way, the Jews had started practicing it as well, and this delineation was powerfully evident in the very layout of Herod's temple in Jerusalem. The temple complex was divided into various courts and sections in Jesus and Paul's day. Some people were allowed to come closer to the actual house of the Lord than others.

Can you imagine walking into your church and being told where you could sit and where you couldn't sit simply because of who you are and how close they think you were allowed to get to the "front" or the "altar"? Can you imagine watching others walking past you each Sunday as they move closer to the front, to the presence of God? What would that do to your heart, soul, and mind? This was exactly what the Gentiles experienced when they visited the temple in Jerusalem in the first century.

When you entered the temple walls, you would have entered the outer court, or the court of the Gentiles. As you looked around, you would have seen an inner wall with pillared columns that were intended to make a stark and bold pronouncement to the Gentiles. The wall served as a stern boundary and barrier to any Gentile seeking to move closer to the house of the Lord. The wall was called the *Soreg*. Excavations in 1871 discovered what is now known as the "Soreg Inscription." Written in Greek, the inscription said something like this:

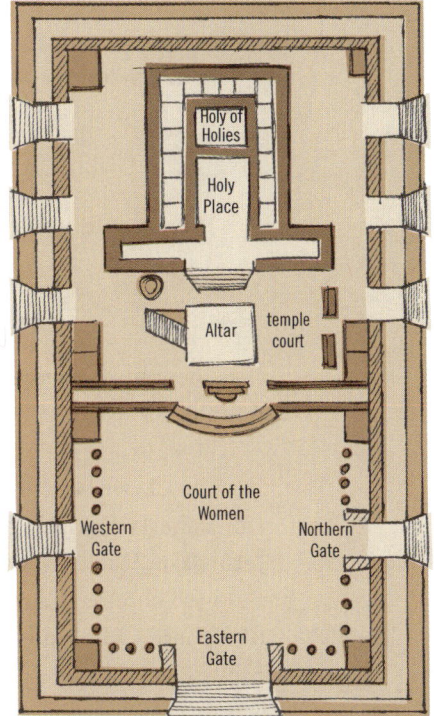

Foreigners must not enter inside the balustrade or into the forecourt around the sanctuary. Whoever is caught will have himself to blame for his ensuing death.[3]

A partial inscription, found in 1936, is located in the Israel Museum today. When I take teams to Israel, we visit this museum and this ancient inscription. A Gentile in Jesus and Paul's world would have been killed if he or she went past the Soreg. Not reprimanded, jailed, or fined—killed.

Kingdom of Togetherness & Empire of Separation

Can you imagine making your long and arduous Gentile pilgrimage to Jerusalem to be met with this inscription? How would you feel?

What would you think about the living God whose house you were standing in as you read it?

What would you do? Leave or stay?

How would you feel as you made the long and arduous journey home?

It is incredibly important to note that the living God did not craft those Soreg boundaries. Man created them. Man did that.

In Acts 21, we read that Trophimus is in Jerusalem; the Bible calls him "Trophimus the Ephesian" (v. 29). We imagine Paul brought Trophimus from Ephesus to Jerusalem. Was he present for the riot in Acts 19? Was he there in the theater while the mob shouted, "Artemis of the Ephesians!" for hours? He came from the world of Ephesus. He came to Jerusalem with Paul. I absolutely *love* that Paul brought him to Jerusalem.

But this caused a kingdom of God ruckus right in the eternal city.

Someone saw Paul at the temple and assumed he had brought Trophimus *past* the Soreg, past the dividing wall that Gentiles weren't allowed to breach. And they said,

> "Fellow Israelites, help us! This is the man who teaches everyone everywhere against our people and our law and this place. And besides, he has brought Greeks into the temple and defiled this holy place." (They had previously seen Trophimus the Ephesian in the city with Paul and assumed that Paul had brought him into the temple.)
> **ACTS 21:28-29**

As you remember from your reading, the Bible goes on to say that "the whole city was aroused" (v. 30). They seized Paul and tried to kill him. The commander of the Roman troops stationed in Jerusalem came to his aid and rescued him by arresting him and placing him in chains.

This kind of fierce turmoil and outburst—all over the possibility that a Gentile walked past the Soreg, the dividing wall. There is such a vast difference between the empire way of separation and the kingdom way of togetherness. Both take energy, but they lead in completely different directions.

We do not know if Paul took Trophimus past the Soreg or not. The Bible doesn't say. But the testimony of his life shows that he believed fiercely in Jews and Gentiles worshiping the living God together, side by side.

For me, the story about Eutychus falling out of the third story window that we read earlier this week is one of the funniest moments in the book of Acts. But this story in Acts 21 challenges and convicts me. Living in the kingdom of togetherness has its challenges. Coming together, cutting across our own ethnic, racial, gender, political, and cultural distinctions requires thoughtful, intentional care and practice. The church is better when she looks more like a bouquet of various flowers rather than twelve red roses. It's the unity in the diversity that speaks so powerfully to this modern, divided world.

> **THE CHURCH IS BETTER WHEN SHE LOOKS MORE LIKE A BOUQUET OF VARIOUS FLOWERS RATHER THAN TWELVE RED ROSES. IT'S THE UNITY IN THE DIVERSITY THAT SPEAKS SO POWERFULLY TO THIS MODERN, DIVIDED WORLD.**

Take a moment to honestly consider where you fall on the spectrum between the kingdom of togetherness and empire of separation when it comes to putting aside ethnic, racial, gender, political, and cultural distinctions. On the following continuum, mark where you are now with an X and mark where you hope to be one day with a circle.

EMPIRE *of* SEPARATION ——————————————— KINGDOM *of* TOGETHERNESS

If you find yourself with room for growth, ask God to help you grow more in unity and togetherness within your local faith family. Pen a prayer below.

I hope we will reach past our modern "Soregs" and dividing walls to experience the diverse flourishing of the kingdom of God on earth as it is in heaven.

session six **learn**

THE GOD OF COMPASSION AND COMFORT

> Yet the LORD longs to be gracious to you; therefore he will rise up to show you compassion. For the LORD is a God of justice. Blessed are all who wait for him!
> **ISAIAH 30:18**

In my role as a college professor, I often tell my students that the Bible was given to us so that we might know who God is—what He's like and what it's like to walk with Him. I encourage them to look for Him in every passage and story in the Bible. This posture with Scripture causes us to look up and out, to open ourselves to seeing His majesty and grandeur while embracing His imminent closeness and proximity to us. The living God is not just "up there and out there." He is also "right here and very near." In theological terms, we call God's majesty and grandeur *transcendence* and His proximity and closeness the *imminence* of the Lord.

The prophet Isaiah told us that the living God rises to show us compassion. In other words, when the Lord longs for something, He longs to be gracious toward you. He longs for it so much that it causes Him to rise up, to get up, and to move toward you to show you compassion. But what is compassion in the biblical world? What does it mean for the Lord to show compassion to us?

We often think of compassion as an emotion. We think of it in terms of how we feel toward someone who is hurting, struggling, grappling, or grieving. Compassion as an emotion is a beautiful thing and much needed in the world.

Kingdom of Togetherness & Empire of Separation

But biblical compassion—the compassion of the living God—is more of a location than just emotion. It's about where you locate yourself in relation to someone who is hurting. The word *compassion* is a fusion of two Greek words: *Com* meaning *with*[4] and *pathos* meaning *suffering*.[5]

Compassion is to be *with* someone *in* his or her pain. It is to locate yourself close and to offer the gift of your presence alongside someone who is hurting, struggling, grappling, or grieving. I think of Isaiah 30:18 often, and I talk about it often. For me, it is one of the most gorgeous verses in the entire Bible because it shows us who God is, what He's like, and what it's like to walk with Him.

The Lord doesn't just feel compassionate emotion toward us. His compassion causes Him to rise up, move toward us, and to locate Himself *with* us *in* our pain. We tend to run from drama. The Lord runs right into it because He knows He can bring *shalom*. He isn't afraid of messy things or messy people. Someone once said, "I may be a mess, but I'm God's mess." The psalmist assured us in Psalm 34:18, "The LORD is close to the brokenhearted and saves those who are crushed in spirit."

Life comes at us hard and fast at times. Pain, hurt, and struggle are part of life in this broken yet being redeemed world. The promise of God's compassionate presence *with* us *in* this world funds our hope. There are many things we don't know, but we know this—we are not alone. And we know this—God comes close, to locate Himself with us in our pain.

The Lord's compassion brings us great comfort. His nearness to us gives us hope. We saw this at the end of Eutychus's story in Acts 20. The people went away from that meal, teaching by Paul, and miracle of God greatly comforted. Why? They had just experienced the powerful presence of the Lord in the raising of Eutychus from the dead. They knew God was with them, among them, working and moving.

READ 2 CORINTHIANS 1:3-7.

The compassion that the Lord gives us teaches us to be compassionate with others. The comfort of the Lord in our lives teaches us how to comfort others. We are invited to give what we've gotten. We are invited to live like rivers and not lakes. As we receive God's compassion, we can be compassionate to others. As we receive the Lord's comfort, we can be comforting to others.

You can't give what you don't have. We need intentional times of being in the presence of the living God to inherit His compassion and comfort. We emerge from it as ambassadors funded and fueled and ready to share it with others. It is one of the most simple yet powerful ways we participate in the restoration, renewal, and repair of all things.

Can you think of a season of your life when you felt the Lord's compassion—Him being with you in your pain? Describe it. Take a moment to thank Him for being steadfast to walk toward you when you're hurting.

Who in your life is compassionate with you? When you hurt, who enters into the pain with you to offer the gift of presence?

Where are you hurting right now? Describe the situation or the pain. Invite the Lord to locate Himself with you right in the hurt. You might even want to write a prayer to Him here.

Who do you know who is hurting right now who needs your gift of presence? Who can you locate yourself with in his/her pain? How will you reach out to him/her this week?

session six **live**

LEARNING TO BELONG

We have learned about some of the regular, scheduled, and calendrical practices and rhythms of the early church. In the Sermon on the Mount, Jesus mentioned three regular practices: generosity, prayer, and fasting (Matt. 6). The early followers of Jesus not only practiced these three things, but they also practiced them together as a community, as a spiritual family.

In sharing these fixed times of table fellowship, prayer, and fasting, they were learning to belong to this new kingdom community. They were learning how to be brothers and sisters in the Lord—sharing their food, sharing their time, sharing their prayers, and fasting together.

Humanity was created to exist in vital, living communion with the living God and with one another. But we have to learn to belong. Throughout life, we learn what it means to be in a family, part of a team, part of a church, and part of a community. It takes time, and it takes intentional practice. Bonding happens when people come together under a common vision, with common purpose and conviction, to share in things together, shoulder-to-shoulder.

I'm an only child, and I have always loved being part of a team. Whether team sports, youth group, serving as a staff member at a church, being part of a non-profit organization, serving as a professor at a college, taking teams overseas, or being part of my spiritual community—I have always gravitated toward doing meaningful things with the meaningful people in my life. It has deeply informed my faith and deeply formed me as a follower of Jesus. I am forever learning to belong—to God and to others.

This week we are going to try and step into the shoes of the early followers of Jesus and actually practice two of these rhythms—fixed times of prayer and fixed days of fasting. We are going to practice "learning to belong" to one another as sisters in the Lord.

HOLY INTERRUPTION

The daily fixed times of prayer and the weekly fixed days of fasting provided something incredibly valuable in the lives of the early followers of Jesus. They both caused holy interruptions in their daily and weekly lives.

When practicing fixed times of prayer, wherever they were, whatever they were doing, whomever they were with, everything ceased at those fixed times so they could pray. It interrupted their work to remind them of God's work—that deep work of bringing restoration, renewal, and repair to the world. Early followers of Jesus knew that their brothers and sisters around the world were praying at the same exact time. When they could not share space, they shared time.

When practicing fixed days of fasting, wherever they were, whatever they were doing, whomever they were with, they abstained from food in solidarity with their brothers and sisters. They were reminded that the true food needed was the food of the soul. Early followers of Jesus knew that their brothers and sisters around the world were fasting on those same days. When they could not share space, they shared time.

We are going to enter into the holy interruption this week. We are going to cease our work to make room for prayer and fasting. We are going to be reminded that God's work, not ours, is the chief work. We are going to be reminded of our need for spiritual food, not just physical food.

For those who want to join us, this week we'll be observing the following fixed times of prayer—9:00 a.m., 12:00 p.m., and 3:00 p.m. At these three times each day, we will stop whatever we are doing, and we will pray the Lord's Prayer. If you are with someone, invite him or her to pray it with you.

For reference, here's what we'll be praying:

> Our Father in heaven,
> hallowed be your name,
> your kingdom come,
> your will be done,
> on earth as it is in heaven.
> Give us today our daily bread.
> And forgive us our debts,
> as we also have forgiven our debtors.
> And lead us not into temptation,
> but deliver us from the evil one.
> **MATTHEW 6:9-13**

For those who want to join us, this week we'll be observing fixed days of fasting on Wednesday and Friday. On Wednesday and Friday this week, we will fast together knowing that our sisters around the country and the world who are participating in this feast are fasting with us.

You can choose to fast from anything. For example, you could fast from your morning cup of coffee, food, social media, or TV. There are so many options, just make sure you fast from something you care about, something you will miss.

For those who choose to join us this week for these special times of prayer and fasting, I pray the holy interruption will bring you great peace, *shalom*, harmony, and wholeness of heart as you are reminded of God's faithful redemptive and restorative work in the earth.

I am so honored to "learn to belong" with you this week. When you go into those times of prayer and fasting, I'll be there with you.

The Long Journey *Home*

HEADED TO THE FATHER'S HOUSE

SESSION SEVEN

Welcome to our seventh and final feast together. It has been an adventure as we have traveled through the book of Acts over the last six sessions. We have seen Jesus's words in Acts 1:8 coming true chapter by chapter, story by story. Acts begins in Jerusalem with Jesus telling His followers that they would be His witnesses in Jerusalem, Judea, Samaria, and unto the ends of the earth. Acts ends with Paul in Rome herself—the imperial city of the Roman Empire.

Everywhere the early followers of Jesus were thrown like seed—often through persecution—the gospel took root and started growing, permeating culture and saturating neighborhoods and cities. And now, the gospel had spread like mustard seed to reach the very heart of the empire.

As C. S. Lewis said: "Enemy occupied territory—that is what this world is. Christianity is the story of how the rightful king has landed, you might say landed in disguise, and is calling us all to take part in a great campaign of sabotage."[1]

We have seen the kingdom of celebration invading the empire of entertainment. We have seen the kingdom of abundance invading the empire of scarcity. We have seen the kingdom of togetherness invading the empire of separation.

We have watched the early followers of Jesus learn to belong to one another in the kingdom of God by practicing table fellowship, generosity, prayer, and fasting together. These kingdom communities located in cities throughout the Roman Empire partnered with the living God to bring restoration, renewal, and repair to the world.

Last week we put ourselves into the shoes of the early followers of Jesus. Many of us practiced fixed times of prayer each day and fixed days of fasting on Wednesday and Friday. This embodied exercise helped us understand some of how they followed the way of Jesus right in the middle of the empire of the Caesars.

This week we will learn how the early followers of Jesus defined and understood "faith." They did not so much speak of having faith, but of "faith-ing" forward. Biblical faith is not only belief but action. We will be encouraged and challenged to faith-forward in our own lives, as the gospel is still moving along the ground through you and me.

Today this gospel-gorgeous story continues.

We will also learn about the *beit av*—the "house of the father" and how this teaching of Jesus traveled with His followers and fueled their vision for what was to come.[2] They were able to endure being thrown like seed throughout the Roman Empire because they carried the promise of Jesus in them that they were headed home. Jesus had promised to come back for them. The rightful King would return, establishing His rule and reign forever and forever. Because of this promise, they did not despise the world of empire but sought to bring light into it.

As we begin our biblical feast, before you watch the video teaching, take a few moments to answer the following questions.

What are the things you learned last week that you have been sharing with others?

If you joined us, how was your experience of practicing the 9:00 a.m., 12:00 p.m., and 3:00 p.m. fixed times of prayer?

If you joined us, how was your experience of fasting on Wednesday and Friday?

How have you lived like a mustard seed, spreading the kingdom of God, this past week?

Have you seen the Lord bring restoration, renewal, and repair to anything or anyone this past week? Where and how?

Watch
SESSION SEVEN

#GospelOnTheGround

THE FEAST

Use the following notes and space provided during our feast-teaching time. Feel free to add your own notes as you watch.

Jesus spent the vast majority of His life within a one-hundred-mile radius of where He was born. Yet His name is spoken and known in every corner of the earth. This is the story of how it happened—and is still happening.

"Our light will outlast their flag."[3]

In the Western world, faith is belief. In the Middle Eastern world, faith is action.

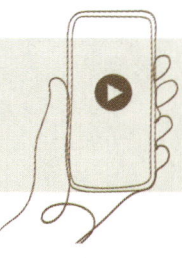

TO ACCESS THE VIDEO TEACHING SESSIONS,
USE THE INSTRUCTIONS IN THE BACK OF YOUR BIBLE STUDY BOOK.

English is a noun-based language. Hebrew is a verb-based language.

Hebrews 11 – "Great Hall of Faith"
It doesn't so much tell us what they believed. It tells us what they did.

Holiness is not the absence of something. Holiness is the presence of something.

Jesus promised that He and His Father were building rooms onto the Father's house. A day is coming when the living God is going to look at His Son and say, "Son, the roooms are ready. Go get Your bride."

session seven **discuss**

LET'S YESHIVA!

Take some time to discuss the following questions with your group:

What did you just hear or see in our feast together that you want to remember?

How would you define holiness? Do you tend to see it more as the absence of something or the presence of something?

What one thing you learned today do you want to share with others this week?

John 14:1-4 is a famous passage for the Christian church. How have you traditionally read and understood Jesus's words here? How do you understand them now?

What is the most surprising thing you learned this week in our video teaching?

What do you imagine Jesus will say to people as they enter the great banquet, the wedding supper of the Lamb?

session seven follow-up

WOMEN IN THE ARENA

Throughout our seven sessions together, we have learned about some of the earliest witnesses of the church. We now know the extra-biblical martyrdom stories of Polycarp and Telemachus along with the biblical martyrdom stories of both Peter and Paul. Others would literally be thrown to wild beasts in arenas located throughout the Roman world. The early church knew that following the way of Jesus in the world of empire would be costly.

These followers of Jesus would perform the way of the kingdom right in the middle of the empire of entertainment. The Roman world gathered in arenas to be entertained with gladiatorial fights, mock naval battles, and horse races. They also witnessed the execution of "criminals" on the arena floor. Sometimes the convicted criminals' crimes were confessing Jesus alone as Lord in the world of the imperial cult. They were considered heretics and atheists in the Roman world.

These brave souls walked onto the arena floor and lived out the way of Jesus right in front of the watching crowd. They would not fight back, strike back, or participate in the games. They demonstrated a lack of fear in the face of death and seemed to die in a manner worthy of the gospel. These arena martyrs were powerful witnesses to the large crowds of Greeks and Romans who were gathered in these arenas. It was one of the largest audiences a follower of Jesus would have ever had in that world, the largest group to embody and proclaim the gospel of Jesus Christ in deed and word.

It is incredibly important to know that women performed the way of the kingdom in the arenas as well. History has preserved a few famous stories of women who gave their lives in gospel-witness in these highly populated arenas. We not only have stories of Polycarp and Telemachus, but we also have the incredible story of Perpetua and Felicity.

> **THESE FOLLOWERS OF JESUS WOULD PERFORM THE WAY OF THE KINGDOM RIGHT IN THE MIDDLE OF THE EMPIRE OF ENTERTAINMENT.**

✳ Arena in Carthage

WOMEN PERFORMED THE WAY OF THE KINGDOM IN THE ARENAS AS WELL.

PERPETUA AND FELICITY

Somewhere between AD 202–205 in Carthage, North Africa, the lives of two women, Perpetua and Felicity, intersected. In the early second century, Carthage rivaled Rome itself. Carthage was a large, bustling, and sophisticated Roman city; she was a jewel of the empire in those days.

Perpetua was a high-born, free Roman woman from a wealthy family. She was well-educated. She would have been expected to marry well and live out her days in the empire of entertainment. She married as a young woman and birthed a son. During that time, she became a follower of Jesus.

Felicity was slave woman within the household of Perpetua's father. She too became a follower of Jesus during the early years of the second-century AD.

Perpetua, Felicity, and others in the household of Perpetua's father were arrested for heresy, for following Jesus, and for not recanting their faith at trial. They were found guilty and sentenced to death in the Carthage arena as criminals. They were jailed and imprisoned together in Carthage. Felicity was pregnant during the time of her arrest and captivity.

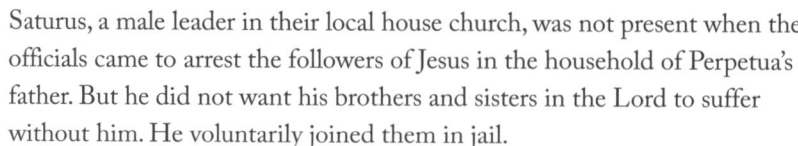

Saturus, a male leader in their local house church, was not present when the officials came to arrest the followers of Jesus in the household of Perpetua's father. But he did not want his brothers and sisters in the Lord to suffer without him. He voluntarily joined them in jail.

Perpetua kept a personal diary. She scribed the details of these events with her own hand. We hear this story from her; we read it in her very own handwriting.

It's a story that calls the church to courage even to this very day.

THE GOSPEL ON THE GROUND

The followers of Jesus—Perpetua, Felicity, Saturus, and other members of the household—spent a few days and nights in the jail with the understanding that they would soon have their day in the arena. In fact, Saturus voluntarily went to jail, likely already knowing that it would mean an appearance in the Carthage arena for him. During their time in jail, Felicity gave birth to a baby girl in the prison.

Two young mothers.

Two followers of Jesus.

One a high-born, free Roman woman. The other, a slave woman.

They performed the way of togetherness in the empire of separation's arena.

In her account, Perpetua wrote that they would all eat their meals together in jail. Local followers of Jesus visited the jail to bring them food and other simple supplies. These early followers of Jesus were sharing table fellowship even in prison. As they ate, they discussed how they wanted to perform the way of the kingdom *in* the arena. They resisted wearing the costumes of the Greek or Roman gods in the arena as criminals often did. These outfits added a theatrical, entertaining value to executions on the arena floor. Perpetua and Felicity wanted to simply stand as followers of Jesus in front of the watching spectators, and they would do it together.

On the eve of their day in the arena, Perpetua gave her diary to a member of their Christian community who had not been arrested. She told him to come to the arena the next day and record what he saw. She wanted their martyrdom stories told to encourage the other followers of Jesus to remain steadfast.

The following day, Saturus, Perpetua, Felicity, and the others entered the arena together. You can read the whole account in *Perpetua's Passion: The Death and Memory of a Young Roman Woman* by Joyce E. Salisbury. A wild cow was unleashed onto the women in the arena, and it knocked Perpetua and Felicity to the ground. As they rose to their feet, they stood in the middle of the arena, holding hands. The empire of separation was shattered by the kingdom of togetherness. Status, family name, and family wealth, or lack thereof, meant nothing in that moment. Two young women. Two young mothers from completely different worlds stood in the heart of the empire of entertainment and showed everyone what the kingdom of God looked like.[4]

All died as martyrs in that arena in Carthage.

The trusted friend that Perpetua gave her diary to was faithful to come to the arena that day and scribe the details of the event. The church at Carthage would read Perpetua's diary annually for centuries to come as a way to remember the story and to be strengthened by it. She bore witness as a martyr in life and death.

The grit and glory of the early church do not belong only to men. Women performed in the arena as well. These are our spiritual foremothers. They have gone before us to show us the way to gain our lives is through losing them.

What is your main takeaway from the story of Perpetua and Felicity?

Prayerfully consider if there are ways that you've chosen the empire of separation over the kingdom of togetherness. Explain.

Is God asking you to be a courageous kingdom witness in any area of your life? Unpack the situation. Consider sharing the request with your small group friends so they can pray with you about it.

session seven **look**

ALL ROADS LEAD TO ROME

*Ancient Roman road and ruins in Ostia Antica

The book of Acts begins in Jerusalem. The book of Acts ends in Rome. Jesus's words had come true—His followers had become witnesses in Jerusalem, Judea, Samaria, and unto the ends of the earth. Acts 28 ends with the apostle Paul living in Rome under house arrest, down the street from NERO , the emperor of the Roman Empire, himself.

We get the feeling that even Rome would not be able to stamp out the gospel within her city limits. The grit and glory of the early church had made it to the imperial city, and the ways of the kingdom would be made known to the way of empire in her most prized and jeweled city.

The Romans built somewhere around fifty thousand miles of paved roads and around two hundred thousand miles in secondary roads. This advancement extended travel throughout the Mediterranean world in ways that had never been seen before. Some of these main thoroughfares and walkways are preserved to this day. Roman roads were typically ten to twelve feet wide and three feet deep. After they dug the trench for the road, it would be filled with layers of tightly packed stones and smaller stones mixed with concrete. The center of the roads was angled a bit higher than the sides so that water would drain off of the roads. The top level of the roadway was paved with flat stones that fit together like a puzzle and pebbles that filled in the gaps.

The vast network of roads and side roads allowed both soldiers and merchants to travel the Empire far and wide. It increased the protection and prosperity of the Roman world. Those same roads also served as the roads that the gospel traveled along through the lives of the followers of Jesus.

The Long Journey Home

* Roman Forum

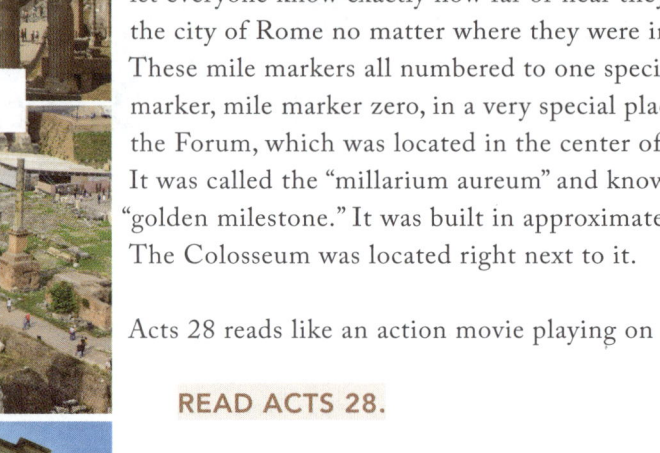

* a Roman *milyon* (mile marker)

We often hear the phrase "all roads lead to Rome." This was not just a cultural statement about the importance of the capital city of the Roman Empire. It was a reality, actualized with the empire's vast road system that included mile markers (*milyons*) set up along the way to let everyone know exactly how far or near they were to the city of Rome no matter where they were in the empire. These mile markers all numbered to one special mile marker, mile marker zero, in a very special place in Rome—the Forum, which was located in the center of the city. It was called the "millarium aureum" and known as the "golden milestone." It was built in approximately 20 BC. The Colosseum was located right next to it.

Acts 28 reads like an action movie playing on fast-forward.

READ ACTS 28.

Pick one of the shorter storylines within the larger story of Acts 28 to unpack further. What passage are you going to be focusing on? List the reference below.

What is the main action in this piece of the story? What's happening?

What does this passage tell you about God—who is He and what He's like?

What does this passage teach you about the early followers of Jesus?

What practical application can you take from this passage? Are there characteristics from the early church that you might want to emulate? How can you embody the way of Jesus based on what you've learned in these verses?

Remember from our study last week, Paul had been arrested in Jerusalem on charges that he took Trophimus the Ephesian past the Soreg, or dividing wall, for Gentiles at the temple. He had appealed to Caesar for his trial because he was a Jew with Roman citizenship. The Jewish officials sent him to Rome to hold court there. According to Acts 27–28, the journey to Rome was incredible; it was a mixture of mishap and miracle, suffering and salvation all along the way.

Paul and his travel companions were shipwrecked on the island of Malta. While there, Paul was bitten by a poisonous viper, miraculously lived through it, and experienced the hospitality of both the islanders and the chief official on the island, named Publius. Publius's father was very sick. Paul prayed for him and healed him. Then the rest of the sick on the island were brought to Paul, and they were all healed too. Mishap and miracle. Suffering and salvation. They do seem to happen side by side in life.

Paul and his travel companions spent three months in Malta. Then they took an Alexandrian ship with Castor and Pollux figureheads (mythological sons of Zeus) to Rome. Once they arrived, brothers and sisters in the Lord from around the city of Rome welcomed them.

In Acts 28, Paul would have walked on one of the most famous Roman roads that led to Rome. It was called the Via Appia; you can still see some of its ruins to this day.

Paul met with the Jewish leaders in Rome and shared the gospel with them. Paul had reached the imperial city, and he would not waste the opportunity.

The Long Journey Home

The Bible tells us,

> [Paul] witnessed to them from morning till evening, explaining about the kingdom of God, and from the Law of Moses and from the Prophets he tried to persuade them about Jesus.
> ACTS 28:23b

The book of Acts ends with two lovely verses. They read like a deep inhale, a hopeful moment of stillness, almost a time to catch your breath in the midst of the whirlwind way that the gospel had been traveling on the ground.

> For two whole years Paul stayed there in his own rented house and welcomed all who came to see him. He proclaimed the kingdom of God and taught about the Lord Jesus Christ—with all boldness and without hindrance!
> ACTS 28:30-31

The mustard seed had not been stamped out, not even in Rome. If Rome cannot stop the gospel spread, what would?

Nothing.

Nothing ever did and nothing has up until now. We are still here. The gospel is still traveling on the ground through you and me. We follow the way of Jesus like Paul and our spiritual ancestors who have gone before us. The "great cloud of witnesses" is cheering us on.

This gospel-gorgeous story continues to this very moment.

We are part of this story and the kingdom of God spreading like a mustard seed.

As followers of Jesus, all roads do *not* lead to Rome. Our path leads to the new Jerusalem—the new Jerusalem promised in Revelation 21–22. We are a people who seek first the kingdom of God and its righteousness. We do not simply want to get to heaven. We want to bring heaven to earth, down to the ground. We agree with Jesus and Paul, we want to bring the kingdom of God to earth as it is in heaven. The new Jerusalem is our home, and it's getting closer every day!

WE ARE PART OF THIS STORY AND THE KINGDOM OF GOD SPREADING LIKE A MUSTARD SEED.

session seven **learn**

RÂDAPH

We have seen the early followers of Jesus thrown like mustard seed throughout the Roman Empire. We have seen the gospel traveling on the ground through the embodied witness and proclamation of the early church. Wherever they went, they proclaimed the kingdom of God. They traveled those thousands of miles of Roman road, sharing the gospel as they went. They endured exile, persecution, being ostracized as heretics and atheists, and being imprisoned, even martyred.

In the midst of it all, they maintained a deep and abiding sense that the living God was with them. They knew that a greater story was being written, that a story greater than the immediate circumstances they found themselves in at any moment would be told. They had learned how to look *through* things, not *at* them. They had learned to see the world of empire with kingdom eyes. No matter what came at them, they knew something deep in their souls.

They knew something was following them.

Râdaph is the Hebrew word for *follow*. It is a strong word that often carries the idea "to pursue," "to chase," even to "to harass" or "to persecute."[5] It can even mean to "chase in order to overtake."[6] When you see the word *râdaph* early in the story of the Bible, it is used with these meanings and imagery.

In Genesis 14, Abram's nephew Lot was captured in Sodom and taken as a prisoner.

When Abram heard the news, he and 318 of his men pursued Lot's captors in order to rescue Lot. They were in hot pursuit, on the chase. It was an aggressive pursuit

The Long Journey Home

in order to overtake Lot's captors. You can feel their energy as Abram contended for his nephew.

> When Abram heard that his relative had been taken captive, he called out the 318 trained men born in his household and went in pursuit as far as Dan. During the night Abram divided his men to attack them and he routed them, pursuing them as far as Hobah, north of Damascus.
> **GENESIS 14:14-15**

In Exodus 14, the Pharaoh of Egypt regretted letting Moses and the Israelites go after the destruction of the ten plagues. He took six hundred plus of his best chariots and soldiers and went after the Israelites to enslave them once more. He was in hot, aggressive pursuit of them as they made their way toward the Red Sea. Again, you can feel the energy in the account. You can almost hear the sound of horses' hooves surging forward and all those chariot wheels churning at full speed.

> The Egyptians—all Pharaoh's horses and chariots, horsemen and troops—pursued the Israelites and overtook them as they camped by the sea near Pi Hahiroth, opposite Baal Zephon.
> **EXODUS 14:9**

As we make our way through the story of the Bible, we come to another place where we see this word *râdaph*. It is found in what we might consider a most unusual place, especially in light of what we've studied up until this point. *Râdaph* is found in a lovely place, a Scripture you may have actually read many times. I'm confident you have heard it before. You may even have it memorized right now in your heart.

In this passage, the word *râdaph* is used in a gospel-gorgeous, beautiful, redeeming way. It still means "to pursue, to chase," and it still carries all the energy of the previous usages we have seen in the Bible. But this time, it's a completely different kind of energy—a different kind of hot pursuit and diligent chase.

Râdaph is found in Psalm 23, the great shepherd psalm. This psalm has comforted, soothed, and calmed our hearts for years. In fact, take a moment to read it again.

READ PSALM 23.

Râdaph occurs in verse 6.

> Surely your goodness and love will follow me all the days of my life, and I will dwell in the house of the LORD forever.
> **PSALM 23:6**

Psalm 23 ends with this beautiful imagery of the goodness and love of God following us. It's in hot pursuit of us. It's chasing us down. It's coming to overtake us, to swallow us up in the goodness and love of God. We do not go looking for the goodness of God—it's coming for us. We do not go looking for the love of God—it's in hot pursuit of us.

The goodness and love of God are nipping at our heels each and every day. No matter what's in front of us—hardship, loss, fear, difficult circumstances—we know what's behind us. When it's scary to look ahead, we can look back. When we look back, we will find story after story, testimony after testimony of how the goodness and love of God have been pursuing and chasing us throughout our lives.

As we live out the way of Jesus together and head toward the new Jerusalem, we are being followed from behind by the goodness and love of God.

How has the goodness and love of God been pursuing you lately?

Can you think of a time when you felt overcome by the goodness and love of God?

What is currently troubling you? Spend some time envisioning His goodness and love in hot pursuit of you right now, today.

The Long Journey Home

session seven **live**

MALCHUT SHAMAYIM

In His earthly ministry, Jesus talked a lot about the kingdom of God (Matt. 4). Jesus taught us to seek first the kingdom of God (Matt. 6), and He said the kingdom of God is like a mustard seed (Matt. 13). The kingdom of God was on Jesus's mind always and was central to His teachings during His earthly ministry. He entered into the world of empire and started proclaiming the kingdom of God, ushering in the *ratzon l'adonai*—the year of the Lord's favor.

The book of Acts begins with the resurrected Jesus in Jerusalem. For forty days, the resurrected Lord showed Himself to His followers. What did He talk about during those forty days?

> He appeared to them over a period of forty days and spoke about the kingdom of God.
> **ACTS 1:3b**

The book of Acts ends with Paul in Rome. For two years he lived in a rented house and welcomed anyone who wanted to come visit him. What did Paul talk about during those two years in Rome?

> He proclaimed the kingdom of God and taught about the Lord Jesus Christ—with all boldness and without hindrance!
> **ACTS 28:31**

The Bible uses two phrases to describe this kingdom, the "kingdom of God" and the "kingdom of heaven." Matthew uses "kingdom of heaven" while Mark and Luke use "kingdom of God."

In Jesus's day and even now, Jews demonstrate respect and honor for God by not saying or pronouncing His name aloud. They use another word as a substitute; they say *heaven*. So through a Middle Eastern lens, the kingdom of heaven and the kingdom of God are the same thing.

The Hebrew phrase for "kingdom of heaven" is **MALCHUT SHAMAYIM**.[7] *Malchut* means *kingdom* and carries the meaning of God's rule, reign, authority, and anyone living under His authority. *Shamayim* means *heavens*. The kingdom of God is anywhere God's rule and reign governs; it's in the life of anyone operating under God's rule.

The kingdom of God is both "now and not yet." It is here, but not fully here—yet. Revelation 21 and 22 show us what it will be like when the kingdom of God is fully realized, when *all* things will be fully and finally brought under the rule and reign of the living God. We taste it now. We know it in part. God's kingdom is anchored in *shalom*, wholeness, flourishing, and delight. But we still live in a fallen, broken, fractured, and sick world.

Part of walking with God and living the way of Jesus as the New Testament church is actively participating with Him to bring the kingdom of God to earth. We want to see His rule and reign increase throughout the earth. We want to see His *shalom*, wholeness, flourishing, and delight move throughout the earth in holiness and power.

We find our purpose as New Testament saints when we partner with Him in bringing restoration, renewal, and repair. The Jewish people call it **TIKKUN OLAM**, the "repair of the world."[8] Forsaking empire and embracing kingdom will cost us. It will probably cost us more than we want to pay. But Jesus showed us that in losing our lives, we actually gain them.

The book of Acts shows us what it looks like to partner with the living God in the *tikkun olam*, the repair of the world. Partnering with God will grant us a gospel-gorgeous life. It may not always be easy, but it will be worth it because He is worth it.

This gospel-gorgeous story continues today.

It continues through you and me.

For years I have had a yellow sticky note on my bathroom mirror. I see it every single morning, and I see it again every single evening. I look at it while I'm getting ready, putting on makeup, or fixing my hair. I have literally looked at it thousands of times, and it speaks to me every single time. I'm not sure I will ever remove it from my bathroom mirror. It may still be there at the end of my life. What does it say?

The reward is on the other side of obedience.

As we end this seven-session feast, it's time to think about how we want to *live* forward from this time together. It's time to trust that God sustains us with His presence in the here and now but brings great reward for those who walk in obedience, who follow His way on the path to *shalom*.

How do you want to participate in the *tikkun olam*?

What do you need to lay down in order to live more fully in the *shalom* of God?

What do you need to pick up in order to live more fully in the *shalom* of God?

Where are you currently witnessing the restoration, renewal, and repair of God?

What is your arena (your areas of relationship or influence)?

How do you want to live the way of the kingdom of God in your arena?

Leader Guide

INTRODUCTION

The Gospel on the Ground is a video- and discussion-based Bible study. The weekly personal study along with the feast-teaching videos will promote honest conversation as you study Scripture together. Since conversation is essential to the experience, you'll find a few starter questions in both the Discuss sections and the Leader Guide to help get the discussion rolling.

This study may be used in a variety of large or small group settings including churches, homes, offices, coffee shops, or other locations according to your needs.

TIPS ON LEADING THIS BIBLE STUDY

PRAY: As you prepare to lead *The Gospel on the Ground*, remember, prayer is essential. Set aside time each week to pray for the women in your group. Listen to their needs and the struggles they're facing so you can bring them before the Lord. Though organizing and planning are important, protect your time of prayer before each gathering. Encourage your women to include prayer as part of their own daily spiritual disciplines as well.

GUIDE: Accept women where they are but also set expectations that motivate commitment. Be consistent and trustworthy. Encourage women to follow through on the study, attend the group sessions, and engage with the personal study. Listen carefully, responsibly guide discussion, and keep confidences shared within the group. Be honest and vulnerable by sharing what God is teaching you throughout the study. Most women will follow your lead and be more willing to share and participate when they see your transparency. Reach out to women of different ages, backgrounds, and stages of life. This variety of experience is sure to make your conversation and time together richer.

CONNECT: Stay engaged with the women in your group. Use social media, emails, text messages, phone calls, or a quick note in the mail to connect with them and share prayer needs throughout the week. Let them know when you are praying specifically for them. Root everything in Scripture and encourage the women in their relationships with Jesus.

CELEBRATE: Leave time at the end of your Session Seven group meeting to celebrate what God has done by having your group share what they've learned and how they've grown. Pray together about any further steps God may be asking them to take as a result of this study.

TIPS ON ORGANIZING THIS BIBLE STUDY

TALK TO YOUR PASTOR OR MINISTER OF EDUCATION OR DISCIPLESHIP: If you're leading this as part of a local church, ask for your leaders' input, prayers, and support.

SECURE YOUR LOCATION: Think about the number of women you can accommodate in the designated location. Reserve tables, chairs, or media equipment for the videos, music, and additional audio needs.

PROVIDE CHILDCARE: If you are targeting moms of young children and/or single moms, childcare will be essential.

PROVIDE RESOURCES: Order the needed number of Bible study books. You might buy a few extra for last-minute sign-ups.

PLAN AND PREPARE: Become familiar with the Bible study resource and leader helps available. Each week you'll watch a video teaching. You'll find detailed information on how to access the videos on the card inserted in the back of the Bible study book. If your group doesn't have adequate internet connection for video streaming, DVD sets are available for purchase at lifeway.com/gospelontheground.

Preview the video session and prepare the outline you will follow to lead the group meeting. Go to lifeway.com/gospelontheground to find free extra leader helps and promotional resources for your study.

EVALUATE

At the end of each group session, ask yourself: *What went well? What could be improved? Did you see women's lives transformed? Did your group grow closer to Christ and to one another?*

NEXT STEPS

Even after the study concludes, follow up and challenge women to stay involved through another Bible study, church opportunity, or ministry to continue their spiritual growth and encourage friendships. Provide several options of ministry opportunities members can participate in individually or as a group to apply what they have learned through this study.

SESSION ONE

1. Welcome your group to the study. Watch the Session One video, using the Watch pages (pp. 16–17), as you come to the weekly feast.

2. Following the video, lead women through the *Yeshiva* group discussion questions (p. 18).

3. Remind the group members to complete the personal study on pages 21–33 at home on their own this week before you meet again.

4. Close the session with prayer.

SESSION TWO

1. Welcome your group to the study. Watch the Session Two video, using the Watch pages (pp. 38–39), and encourage the women to take notes as Kristi teaches.

2. Following the video, lead women through the *Yeshiva* group discussion questions (p. 40).

3. Remind the group members to complete the personal study on pages 43–58 at home on their own this week before you meet again.

4. Close: Challenge women to consider how they might intentionally take part in the kingdom of celebration. Brainstorm some ideas together. For example, women might invite someone to dinner, send a note of encouragement to a friend, meet a need in the community, or take extra time in prayer and worship this week.

SESSION THREE

1. Welcome your group to the study. Watch the Session Three video, using the Watch pages (pp. 64–65), and encourage the women to take notes as Kristi teaches.

2. Following the video, lead women through the *Yeshiva* group discussion questions (p. 66).

3. Remind the group members to complete the personal study on pages 69–83 at home on their own this week before you meet again.

4. Close: Ask women to form groups of two to four people and share any doubts or challenges that may keep them from fully embracing the joy and security of living in the "year of the Lord's favor." Instruct them to pray for each other after they've shared.

SESSION FOUR

1. Welcome your group to the study. Watch the Session Four video, using the Watch pages (pp. 88–89), and encourage the women to take notes as Kristi teaches.

2. Following the video, lead women through the *Yeshiva* group discussion questions (p. 90).

3. Remind the group members to complete the personal study on pages 93–107 at home on their own this week before you meet again.

4. Close: Take some time to discuss people you know whose lives are marked by generosity in the way they treat others. Explain what about these people tells others they're generous. Close the time in prayer, thanking God for the abundance that can be found in His kingdom and asking Him to help the women in your group rest secure in His love, care, and provision for them.

SESSION FIVE

1. Welcome your group to the study. Watch the Session Five video, using the Watch pages (pp. 112–113), and encourage the women to take notes as Kristi teaches.

2. Following the video, lead women through the *Yeshiva* group discussion questions (p. 114).

3. Remind the group members to complete the personal study on pages 117–133 at home on their own this week before you meet again.

4. Close: Break up into smaller groups and discuss the last two *Yeshiva* questions, "What are your current table fellowship practices and how can you be more intentional to use your dining room as an instrument for the kingdom of God?" Give space and time for women to share barriers and struggles they may face when it comes to hosting. Instruct women to close their time together by praying for one another.

SESSION SIX

1. Welcome your group to the study. Watch the Session Six video, using the Watch pages (pp. 138–139), and encourage the women to take notes as Kristi teaches.

2. Following the video, lead women through the *Yeshiva* group discussion questions (p. 140).

3. Remind the group members to complete the personal study on pages 143–158 at home on their own this week before you meet again.

4. Close: For women who are willing to take part in the fixed times of prayer and fasting this week, make a plan to check in with each other during the week to encourage one another and ask how it's going. (Make sure not to pressure women who are unable or unwilling to participate.) Close the time in prayer, asking God to unify your small group in your love for Him and one another.

SESSION SEVEN

1. Welcome your group to the study. Watch the Session Seven video, using the Watch pages (pp. 164–165), and encourage the women to take notes as Kristi teaches.

3. Following the video, lead women through the *Yeshiva* group discussion questions (p. 166).

4. Remind the group members to complete the personal study on pages 169–182.

5. Close: Take a few minutes to celebrate what God has done in your group over these seven sessions. Now that you've studied many of the early church's stories, how do you sense God calling you to live like a mustard seed and partner with Him in bringing restoration, renewal, and repair to the world—as an individual and as a community of faith?

Acts Reading Plan

The book of Acts gives us a beautiful snapshot of the early church—both its challenges and its joys. During our time together, we'll highlight many passages from the book of Acts, but a comprehensive, verse-by-verse study of the book of Acts is not within the scope of this study. If you'd like to take the time to read the entire book of Acts as you're walking through our study of *The Gospel on the Ground*, we've provided a supplementary reading plan for you below. Happy reading!

SESSION ONE

- ☐ Acts 1
- ☐ Acts 2
- ☐ Acts 3
- ☐ Acts 4

SESSION TWO

- ☐ Acts 5
- ☐ Acts 6
- ☐ Acts 7
- ☐ Acts 8

SESSION THREE

- ☐ Acts 9
- ☐ Acts 10
- ☐ Acts 11
- ☐ Acts 12

SESSION FOUR

- ☐ Acts 13
- ☐ Acts 14
- ☐ Acts 15
- ☐ Acts 16

SESSION FIVE

- ☐ Acts 17
- ☐ Acts 18
- ☐ Acts 19
- ☐ Acts 20

SESSION SIX

- ☐ Acts 21
- ☐ Acts 22
- ☐ Acts 23
- ☐ Acts 24

SESSION SEVEN

- ☐ Acts 25
- ☐ Acts 26
- ☐ Acts 27
- ☐ Acts 28

Endnotes

INTRODUCTION

1. Strong's H3389, Bible Hub, https://biblehub.com/hebrew/3389.htm.
2. C. S. Lewis, *Mere Christianity* (New York: HarperCollins: 1952), 46.
3. Ibid.

SESSION ONE

1. Rabbi Jonathan Sacks, "The Far Horizon (Bo 5781)," January 18, 2021, jonathansacks.org. https://rabbisacks.org/bo-5781/.
2. Deborah E. Lipstadt, "What Does Bar Mitzvah mean?," My Jewish Learning, https://www.myjewishlearning.com/article/what-does-bar-mitzvah-mean/.
3. Phil Hopersberger, "The Southern Steps," Israel: Land of Creation, http://www.land-of-the-bible.com/The_Southern_Steps.
4. Dr. James Emery White, "40: God's Number for Life Change," Crosswalk, Salem Web Network, February 18, 2021, https://www.crosswalk.com/blogs/dr-james-emery-white/40-gods-number-for-life-change.html.
5. Strong's H4687, Blue Letter Bible, https://www.blueletterbible.org/lexicon/h4687/kjv/wlc/0-1/.
6. Tzvi Freeman, "What Is a Mitzvah?," Chabad.org, https://www.chabad.org/library/article_cdo/aid/1438516/jewish/Mitzvah.htm.

SESSION TWO

1. Strong's H8527, Blue Letter Bible, https://www.blueletterbible.org/lexicon/h8527/kjv/wlc/0-1/.
2. John Gill, *John Gill's Exposition of the Bible*, accessed via Bile Study Tools, 1746–1748, https://www.biblestudytools.com/acts/2-1.html.
3. Strong's H8548, Blue Letter Bible, https://www.blueletterbible.org/lexicon/h8548/kjv/wlc/0-1/.
4. M. Grant, "Augustus," *Encyclopedia Britannica*, August 15, 2021, https://www.britannica.com/biography/Augustus-Roman-emperor.
5. F. Pohl, "Tiberius," *Encyclopedia Britannica*, March 12, 2021. https://www.britannica.com/biography/Tiberius.
6. G. Suetonius Tranquillus, *The Twelve Caesars*, trans. Alexander Thomson, reprint, 2011.
7. Protagoras, *Stanford Encyclopedia of Philosophy*, "Man is the measure of all things," https://plato.stanford.edu/entries/protagoras/.
8. Ibid., Lewis.
9. Hila Ratzabi, "What Was the Tabernacle (Mishkan)?," My Jewish Learning, https://www.myjewishlearning.com/article/the-tabernacle/.
10. Dietrich Bonhoeffer, *Dietrich Bonhoeffer: Witness to Jesus Christ, The Making of Modern Theology series*, ed. John 1. De Gruchy (Minneapolis, First Fortress Press, 1991), 187.
11. Pierre Teilhard de Chardin, *Hearts on Fire* (Chicago: Loyola Press, 2005), 102–103.

SESSION THREE

1. Rabbi Abraham Joshua Heschel, *God in Search of Man: A Philosophy of Judaism* (New York: Farrar, Straus and Giroux, 1955), 34.
2. "Sepphoris—The Forgotten City," Land of the Bible, https://www.land-of-the-bible.com/Sepphoris_The_Forgotten_City.
3. Ibid.
4. Strong's G5045, Blue Letter Bible, https://www.blueletterbible.org/lexicon/g5045/kjv/tr/0-1/.
5. Robby Gallaty, "Was Jesus a Carpenter or a Stonemason?," *The Christian Post*, April 29, 2017, https://www.christianpost.com/news/jesus-carpenter-or-stonemason.html.
6. "Sepphoris—The Forgotten City."
7. Strong's H7522, Blue Letter Bible, blueletterbible.org/lexicon/h7522/kjv/wlc/0-1/.
8. Strong's H136, Blue Letter Bible, https://www.blueletterbible.org/lexicon/h136/kjv/wlc/0-1/.

SESSION FOUR

1. Strong's H1818, Blue Letter Bible, https://www.blueletterbible.org/lexicon/h1818/kjv/wlc/0-1/.
2. Mishnah Sanhedrin 4:5, accessed via https://www.sefaria.org/English_Explanation_of_Mishnah_Sanhedrin.4.5.3?lang=bi&with=all&lang2=en.
3. Bob Goff, *Live in Grace*, Walk in Love (Nashville: Nelson Books, 2019), 50.
4. Strong's G3144, Blue Letter Bible, https://www.blueletterbible.org/lexicon/g3144/kjv/tr/0-1/.
5. Tim Keller, as quoted in J.R. Briggs's book *The Sacred Overlap: Learning to Live Faithfully in the Space Between* (Grand Rapids, MI: Zondervan, 2020).
6. Jerome, "Letter 77," accessed via New Advent, https://www.newadvent.org/fathers/3001077.htm.
7. Strong's G3144.

8. The Editors of *Encyclopedia Britanica*, "Gamaliel I," *Encyclopedia Britannica*, July 20, 1998, https://www.britannica.com/biography/Gamaliel-I
9. Terrence Malick, director, *A Hidden Life*, 2019, Searchlight Pictures.
10. Strong's G1131, Blue Letter Bible, https://www.blueletterbible.org/lexicon/g1131/nasb20/mgnt/0-1/.
11. Strong's G4712, Blue Letter Bible, https://www.blueletterbible.org/lexicon/g4712/kjv/tr/0-1/.
12. Strong's G3144.

SESSION FIVE

1. *Merriam-Webster*, s.v. "History of Companion," https://www.merriam-webster.com/dictionary/companion.
2. Pliny, Letters 10.96-97, accessed via Georgetown.edu, https://faculty.georgetown.edu/jod/texts/pliny.html#:~:text=Meanwhile%2C%20in%20the%20case%20of,who%20persisted%20I%20ordered%20executed.
3. Strong's G4635, Blue Letter Bible, https://www.blueletterbible.org/lexicon/g4635/kjv/tr/0-1/.
4. Strong's G5045, Blue Letter Bible, https://www.blueletterbible.org/lexicon/g5045/kjv/tr/0-1/.
5. *Merriam-Webster,* s.v. "guild," https://www.merriam-webster.com/dictionary/guild.
6. Gene A. Getz and Jim Moore, *Men of Character: Paul* (Nashville, TN: B&H Books, 2000).
7. Strong's H7522.
8. Strong's H136.
9. Cornelius Plantinga, Jr., *Not the Way It's Supposed to Be* (Grand Rapids, MI: William B. Eerdmans Publishing Company, 1995).

SESSION SIX

1. J. Lee Grady, *Follow Me* (Lake Mary, FL: Charisma Media, 2022), 17.
2. Strong's G2161, Blue Letter Bible, https://www.blueletterbible.org/lexicon/g2161/kjv/tr/0-1/.
3. "Temple Warning Inscription," Holy Land Photos, http://holylandphotos.org/browse.asp?s=1,3,7,202,203,336,337&img=TWMRISAM06.
4. Merriam-Webster, s.v. "History of Companion."
5. *Merriam-Webster*, s.v. "pathos," https://www.merriam-webster.com/dictionary/pathos.

SESSION SEVEN

1. Ibid., Lewis.
2. Shoshana Kordova, "Word of the Day / Beit Av: It's a Dad's World," My Jewish Learning, October 20, 2013, https://www.haaretz.com/.premium-word-of-the-day-beit-av-1.5276398#:~:text=Beit%20av%20literally%20means%20%E2%80%9Chouse,is%20also%20called%20meshek%20bayit).
3. "A Jewish Hanukkah menorah defies the Nazi swastika, 1931," Rare Historical Photos, Oct. 14, 2017, https://rarehistoricalphotos.com/menorah-defies-nazi-flag/.
4. Joyce E. Salisbury, *Perpetua's Passion: The Death and Memory of a Young Roman Woman* (New York and London: Taylor & Francis, 2013).
5. Strong's H7291, Blue Letter Bible, https://www.blueletterbible.org/lexicon/h7291/kjv/wlc/0-1/.
6. "Radaph," Brown-Driver-Briggs, https://biblehub.com/hebrew/7291.htm.
7. Ronald J. Allen and Clark M. Williamson, *Preaching the Old Testament: A Lectionary Commentary* (Louisville, London: Westminster John Knox Press, 2007), 81.
8. "Tikkun Olam: Repairing the World," My Jewish Learning, https://www.myjewishlearning.com/article/tikkun-olam-repairing-the-world/.ufzRDwAAQBAJ?hl=en&gbpv=1&dq=tamid+-sacrifice+%229+a.m.%22&pg=PA1897&printsec=-frontcover

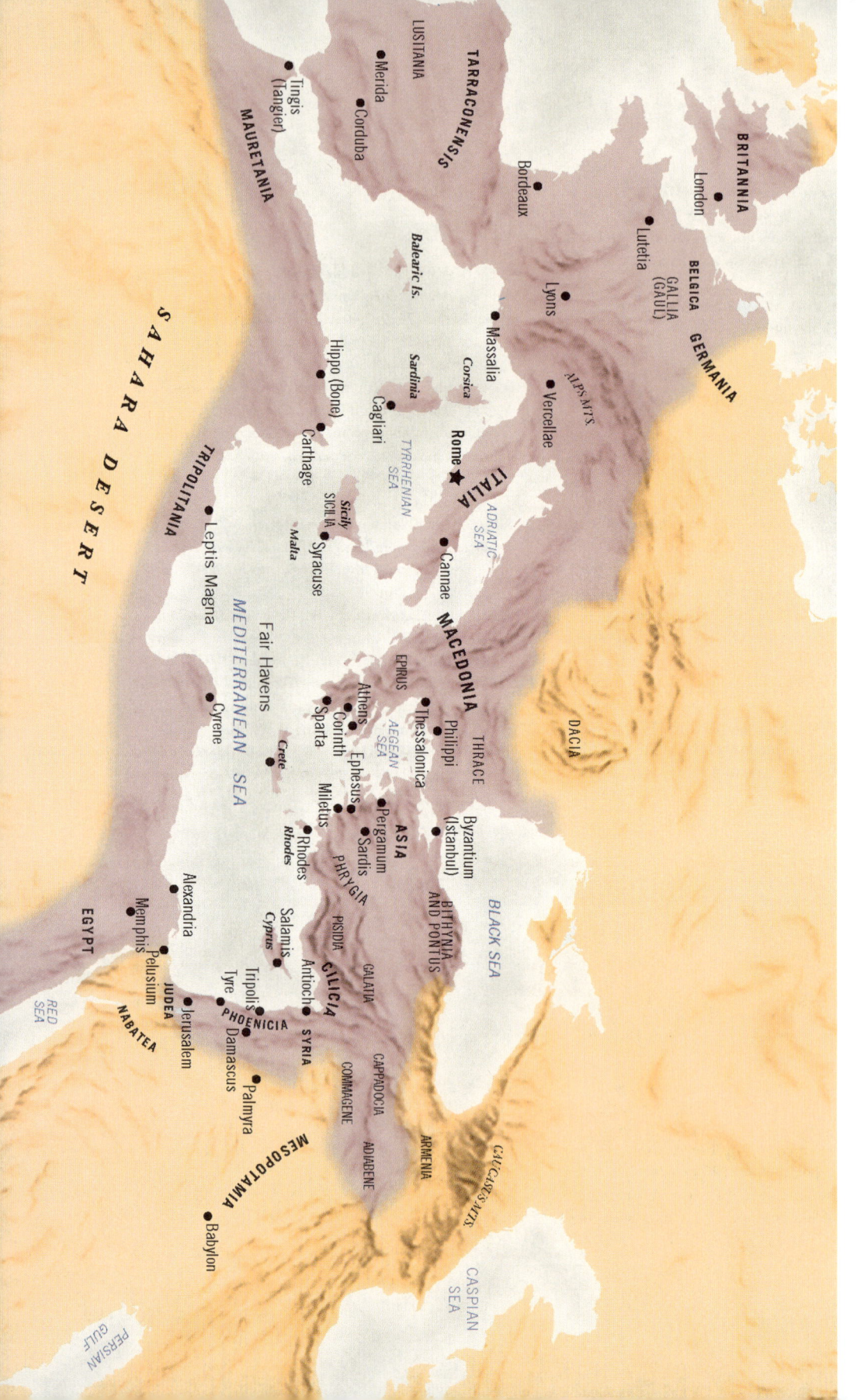

Take heart, daughter.

Matthew 9:22

Imagine walking the dusty roads of Galilee with Jesus of Nazareth—braving jostling crowds just to touch the edge of His cloak and hear Him say, "Take heart, daughter, your faith has healed you."

Those words, once meant to comfort a hurting woman's soul thousands of years ago, were also meant for you.

Join biblical culturalist Kristi McLelland on those dusty roads as she transports you back to Jesus' world, stepping into the footsteps of the women who came face to face with the living God. Over 7 sessions, examine the historical and cultural climate of first-century Middle Eastern society to not only understand Jesus more deeply but to fuel your worship of Him today.

lifeway.com/jesusandwomen | 800.458.2772

lifeway. women

Pricing and availability are subject to change without notice.

Get the most from your study.

Customize your Bible study time with a guided experience.

In this study, you'll:

- See how God's redemptive purposes are unstoppable in the book of Acts.
- Gain deeper insight into the biblical world, including fresh perspective on familiar Bible stories.
- Ignite a passion to be on mission by examining the work of the early church.
- Find deep purpose and meaning at the table of God.

Watching Kristi's video teaching sessions is essential to experiencing the full learning impact of the study. Each 50-60-minute video teaching unpacks fundamental truths and clarifies study questions found in *The Gospel on the Ground* Bible study book.

STUDYING ON YOUR OWN?

Watch Kristi's teaching sessions as you study, available via redemption code printed in your Bible study book.

LEADING A GROUP?

Each group member will need a *The Gospel on the Ground* Bible Study Book, which includes video access. Because all participants will have access to the video content, you can choose to watch the videos outside of your group meeting if desired. Or, if you're watching together and someone misses a group meeting, she'll have the flexibility to catch up! A DVD set is also available to purchase separately if desired.

ALSO AVAILABLE

DVD Set includes 2 DVDs with 7 teaching videos from Kristi McLelland, approximately 50-60 minutes per session

Teen girls' Bible study book, 7-session study

Browse study formats, a free session sample, video clips, church promotional materials, and more at

lifeway.com/gospelontheground

Here's Your Video Access.

To stream *The Gospel on the Ground* Bible study video teaching sessions, follow these steps:

1. Go to my.lifeway.com/redeem and register or log in to your Lifeway account.

2. Enter this redemption code to gain access to your individual-use video license:

Once you've entered your personal redemption code, you can stream the video teaching sessions any time from your Digital Media page on my.lifeway.com or watch them via the Lifeway On Demand app on any TV or mobile device via your Lifeway account.

There's no need to enter your code more than once! To watch your streaming videos, just log in to your Lifeway account at my.lifeway.com or watch using the Lifeway On Demand app.

QUESTIONS? WE HAVE ANSWERS!
Visit support.lifeway.com and search "Video Redemption Code" or call our Tech Support Team at 866.627.8553.

This video access code entitles you to one non-transferable, single-seat license with no expiration date. Please do not share your code with others. Videos are subject to expiration at the discretion of the publisher. Do not post Bible study videos to YouTube, Vimeo, any social-media channel, or other online services for any purpose. Such posting constitutes copyright infringement and is prohibited by the terms of use. Unauthorized posting also violates the service rules, which can negatively affect your YouTube or other service account.